URBAN SURVIVAL
GUIDE

URBAN SURVIVAL GUIDE

How City Dwellers Can Live Well, and Frugally, Even in Dire Times

CHRISTOPHER NYERGES

Skyhorse Publishing

Skyhorse Publishing books may be purchased in bulk at special discounts for sales promotion, corporate gifts, fund-raising, or educational purposes. Special editions can also be created to specifications. For details, contact the Special Sales Department, Skyhorse Publishing, 307 West 36th Street, 11th Floor, New York, NY 10018 or info@skyhorsepublishing.com.

Skyhorse® and Skyhorse Publishing® are registered trademarks of Skyhorse Publishing, Inc.®, a Delaware corporation.

Visit our website at www.skyhorsepublishing.com.

10 9 8 7 6 5 4 3 2 1

Library of Congress Cataloging-in-Publication Data is available on file.

Cover design by Kai Texel
Cover photo credits: Christopher Nyerges, Dave Strom (electronics photo)

Print ISBN: 978-1-5107-6173-5
Ebook ISBN: 978-1-5107-6315-9

Printed in China

TABLE OF CONTENTS

DEDICATION

Dedicated to Richard E. White, and to Henry David Thoreau.

This book is also dedicated to my many mentors who took their time to answer my questions and to allow me a peek into their lifestyles.

ACKNOWLEDGMENTS

The gestation of this book took a long time, and there were many people who provided inspiration, as well as the hard data that a book like this requires.

I want to acknowledge Richard E. White for the long hours he spent with me discussing the many principles that are found in this book. His very life was inspirational to me.

I thank Steve Lamb and Keith Farrar for some of the details in this book, as well as Dr. James Adams, and Enrique Villasenor, whose stories I was able to tell in this book. For their participation, I also thank Matt Heidrich, Jay Hartman, Kia Bordner, Oscar Duardo, Miguel and Dennis Hernandez, Steve Lamb, Francisco Loaiza, Shawn Maestretti, Dave Strom, Kevin Sutherland, and Dorothy Wong.

Thank you Jane Tsong for your thoughts and ideas about how we all ought to be living our urban lives in a more sustainable manner.

I extend my appreciation to all the others who have walked this path with me, and joined me in conversations, workshops, classes, and problem-solving sessions: Gary Gonzales, Angelo Cervera, James Ruther, Rick and Karen Adams, Helen Sweany, Prudence Daniel, Julie Balaa, Talal Balaa, David Martinez, Timothy Hall, David Ashley, and others. Thank you my dear Helen for assisting me on this path!

Christopher Nyerges

FOREWORD

Christopher Nyerges has honed self-reliance to an art, not only to survive a disaster, but as a way of life. Equally at home in the city as in the wilderness, his life is an ongoing quest to thrive on less.

During the '70s, I could not find backpacking gear in my size (being seven feet tall), so I taught myself how to make a lightweight sleeping bag, an all-weather jacket, and a pair of hiking and cross-country ski boots. A decade later, married with two children, I was growing enough vegetables to feed our family. But I never managed to bring down our utility bills and we always remained a high-input household. It takes discipline and dedication to disentangle ourselves from the consumer society.

The evolution of civilization is a process of increasing specialization and interdependence. Not only does every individual depend on a large number of specialists to live in comfort, but nowadays whole countries get in trouble during an interruption in global trade. Add to that modern management's preoccupation with efficiency and the tight coupling of dependencies such as "just-in-time" to minimize inventory costs, and our vulnerability to any kind of natural disaster becomes even more pronounced. The shortages of protective equipment during the coronavirus pandemic is at least partly a result of this eagerness to maximize efficiency.

Every so often we need to be reminded of the likelihood of a natural disaster. Here in California, a major earthquake could disrupt electricity, water, internet, and mobile phone services for an extended time. The devastation could be so extreme and widespread that we will find ourselves in need of some basic survival skills.

In this book, Christopher shows us the many ways by which we can reduce our reliance on the trappings of modern living and thereby become more resilient in case of a natural disaster. Many of us may only be able to implement a few of Christopher's many suggestions, but the book will serve as a lifelong reference and inspiration.

— *Carel Struycken, actor and proponent of permaculture*

INTRODUCTION

On the path to a sustainable life … in the city

Back a million years ago when I was in high school, my days were spent engrossed in the study of mycology, botany, and herbalism. Through the ancient knowledge of the use of wild plants, I saw the very salvation of the world that everyone else seemed to have forgotten and left behind.

I was still young, and not caught up in making money as the primary purpose and goal of my life. I truly thought that the problem with modern society was that there was something that "we" were all missing, or ignoring.

I moved to my grandfather's farm in rural Ohio, since I believed that perhaps the methods built into farm living somehow imparted the simplicity and natural self-reliance I was seeking. But—in general—I found that farm people were just like everyone else in wanting the latest gadgets and technological devices as the main means to improve life. I saw some hope and solace in observing the rites of the Amish, who eschewed electricity and insisted on a life full of manual labor and community involvement. It did not hurt their goals to have large farms and large open spaces where they lived. Still, I was an outsider to the Amish. I wondered if their methods were possible to apply if I did not have a large farmstead, and a large group of like-minded neighbors.

When I returned to California, I was introduced to Richard White, who had recently founded a non-profit (White Tower Inc., or WTI), whose purpose was to teach city dwellers how to live their daily lives more ecologically. The *raison d'être* of his organization was to learn, study, live, and share techniques of wilderness survival, urban survival, economic survival, political survival, physical survival, and spiritual survival. He was a pioneer in this broad approach to life, and he took more than his share of criticism. I became his student, joined his organization, and let his influence dominate my thinking about the ways I could live more frugally, and get more for less.

Along the way, I learned many abiding principles that I've more or less followed all of my life. In both his private and public life, White was a radical minimalist, one who believed that it was best (physically, morally, spiritually) to not waste resources, and to use only those resources that you actually need. He completely embodied the Depression-era motto by Boyd K. Packer, to "Use it up, wear it out, make it do, or do without."

I believe that if there had ever been a serious catastrophe where he lived during his lifetime, he would have continued his daily routine, more or less unhampered. Such was the degree of his minimalism. It is from my interactions with White that many of the lessons of this book derive.

As a part of my involvement with White's non-profit, I was introduced to another pioneer, Marshall Greenwood, about whom an article had been written in the *Los Angeles Times*. Greenwood was described as "America's Greatest Poor Man," and he wrote a book describing his lifestyle and how he managed to live on $99 a month in his San Diego apartment. In the writings of Greenwood, I found a like-minded person who described the folly of so many of the products of modern life which so many people believe they cannot live without. Greenwood lived a good life without having to pay for all the stuff he considered nonessential. In fact, he discovered—in much the way that Thoreau discovered, as I have discovered—that many of the trappings of modern life keep us very busy being very busy. They keep us too distracted to live life fully and too often keep us from living our life to its fullest potential. We mistake acquiring a lot of stuff for a truly meaningful and successful life.

At this time, I was living in Pasadena, practiced organic gardening in the side yard, and bicycled most of the time. I was a student of botany, mycology, and journalism at the local college. Soon, I moved into northeast Los Angeles, and worked more actively with White's new non-profit, and taught inner-city youth such skills as fence building, framing small structures, gardening, and landscaping. In that capacity, I became aware of an empty house on a one-acre lot in that neighborhood. I occupied that house, fixed it up, and squatted there for a year and a half. As a result of that unique situation, I used the opportunity to practice low-impact self-reliant living. I grew some of my food, and raised some animals. I practiced composting, and used a small woodstove for some of my cooking. I learned to make usable furniture from discarded wood, and I collected and used rainwater. All these things I did because I wanted to practice living lightly on the land. I worked all the time, though since I only had a few part-time jobs, all my practices were very much low-budget. In fact, to be accurate, they were "no-budget."

That was over forty years ago, and a lot has happened since then as I have continued to seek and find ways to live a low-cost ecological lifestyle. It has never been my intent to do these things in order to coerce others to change their lifestyles. I was concerned about my own personal choices, and the impact of my choices upon the environment. If others found some value in what I did, I always found that to be a good thing. However, I mostly heard (usually third-hand) the negative comments. These included, "What he does is very impractical," or, "He wouldn't need to do those things if he just got a job," and even, "He's a bum." Yes, I understand such feelings.

As I understood from the descendants of the peers of Thoreau, he was by no means admired during his lifetime. Rather, he was regarded as somewhat lazy, a bum, and someone who would not, or could not, hold a job. Thoreau was seen as someone who would rather hang out in the woods with the Indians rather than working at some job in town. Only today is Thoreau's simplicity valued by school teachers and intellectuals who wish to capture those lessons of self-reliance for a modern generation.

White was well aware of the ravages caused to the earth by everyone's voracious appetite for more and more stuff. He often used the excesses of the Christmas season to make his point, namely, how we rush about on crowded highways, buying lots of stuff that we can barely afford, in the hopes of abiding by the societal norm of giving things to other people. Should we actually be commemorating what should be a Holy Time by this excess of wanton consumerism?

Once, during one of his educational exercises, we dumped a post-Christmas trash can and analyzed the items that are routinely and casually tossed away. At least half was packaging, mostly paper-based, and now just wasted. The other half consisted of products that could still be used, or recycled, but are now just discarded. These were items manufactured from wood, paper, plastic, glass, metal, and maybe fabric. We took our time to discuss what it took for our society to get to the point that such valuable products could be manufactured for our ease, and we discussed the ramifications on the environment to produce such products merely to discard them into landfills. We came to see how our buying habits were part of the worldwide trash problem, and degradation of the environment.

Since a big component of White's non-profit was "spiritual survival" (he also emphasized physical survival, wilderness survival, emotional survival, mental survival, moral survival, and economic survival), we looked at each discarded item from the standpoint of Karma.

By Karma—the Law of Cause and Effect—White was intending for each of his mentees to take responsibility for any and all resources that they came into contact with, a goal that most regarded as "impractical." The short version of this is that we create our own destinies by our millions of choices, including how we use resources. "If you waste water," he told us, "you will find yourself—sooner or later—in a situation with no water, or less than you need." That could manifest as drought, toxic water from fracking, or even inability to pay the water bill. Though he often spoke about the effects that industry has on the lives of many (fouled air, water, and land), he emphasized that the way to improve our status is to improve the quality of our personal and private choices.

This book arose from several of my experiences: The most important influence was Richard White and the positive but frugal urban lifestyle he lived and taught. I was also a squatter for a year and a half in the city of Los Angeles, and took many West Coast hitch-hiking trips and numerous camping trips throughout the Southwest. It was my great desire to live off the land like the great homesteaders of a century earlier. All of these experiences influenced my point of view as to why we have the economical and environmental problems we have, and how the solution begins with our personal choices.

SOME PERSONAL BACKGROUND

I was a squatter between 1977 into 1979, when I experimented and learned much about urban animal husbandry, raising food, wild foods, alternatives to conventional power sources, alternatives to the flush toilet, and so on.

During this time, after I had met Richard White, the combination of my experiences led me to the insight that the primary reason we are still facing an ecological crisis is because we are not collectively choosing a lifestyle that is compatible with environmental health. It is not very complicated!

I was able to live well on less, while experimenting with food and power production, recycling, and gardening. In moments of reflection—usually late at night—I realized that most urban dwellers rush through the best part of their lives to make money at their job, to support a non-ecological home and lifestyle that simply further exacerbates all our economic and ecological problems. Most often, these choices are made because there seem to be no other options, and so millions work in big cities when they'd rather live elsewhere, so they'd be close to the job that enables them to support the lifestyle that they'd rather not have.

Though many books had been written on how to move to a rural area and become self-sufficient there, few practical guidebooks had been written for the urban dweller who also wants to live ecologically and be a part of the solution. In fact, perhaps most city dwellers don't really have the option to move to a rural environment.

When the idea for this book first arose, it was intended that it would provide a basic blueprint for the average city dweller to become more self-reliant. It was intended to provide simple choices for anyone who wanted to be a part of the solution. All of the ideas and choices were to be within the existing social structure, legal, simple, and economical. In other words, my associates and I wanted every reader to say, "Hey, I can do that *today*, in my own kitchen, or backyard, and it doesn't cost me anything!" We wanted every reader to realize that there was, and is, nothing to wait for, and no need to sit around hoping "the government" does something.

An early, very different version of this book was released in 1980, and yet another version was created 1998, when we were getting lots of calls from worried people who were being told that the world would end when 2000 rolled around due to the Y2K computer problem.

We started doing research, and were pretty certain that the world was not going to come to an end at the end of 1999. Still, we found ourselves telling people to do all the things that they should do to prepare for a major earthquake. That is, store food and water, have medical supplies, cooking supplies, a simple toilet in the backyard, cash on hand, a woodstove, solar panels, and so on.

If the worst-case Y2K scenario was to come to pass, it would be like a major earthquake disrupting everything, but the buildings would still be standing!

We soon found ourselves fielding so many queries that we started conducting seminars to reassure city people that the world would not end and that there were positive actions they could take.

When January 2000 rolled around, no one was interested in Y2K anymore, but all the basic details of self-reliant living found in this book were—and are—still valid and viable: an efficient living shelter, water, food, cooking, hygiene, alternatives to electricity, communications, wise use of resources, community and safety, and how we live our lives.

The Great Tsunami of Christmas 2004 showed us that quick extinctions (like Noah's flood) can and do happen without apparent warning. Hurricane Katrina not only told us that it can happen to us, but that it is foolhardy to make no preparations and pretend that the government will take care of you in the post-disaster landscape. War, rumors of war, famines, political instability, economic instability, viruses and biological contamination, the Four Horsemen of the Apocalypse, the Beast—all these real and fictional issues are causes for concern to the average family.

As I write this, everyone is still reeling over the coronavirus pandemic of 2020, wondering whether government actions made things worse, or made things better. Whatever is finally determined, it's good to keep in mind that you can never prepare for everything. This is partly due to the fact that the thing that eventually gets you is the very thing that you had not even considered!

Still, this is not a book about surviving a disaster. This is a book for simple living, with a focus on city living. Part of this simple living includes the topic of "economic survival" since this is such a fundamental building block of everything else in modern society. Money cannot be ignored.

THOREAU REVISITED

Remember, what you are about to read will include many of my ideas and perspectives, but at the end of the day, this is all about the basic principles of living ecologically and economically—in the city! The city is where most of us live, like it or not. And when I try to get into Thoreau's mind, I realize that, in essence, he just walked to the edge of his town and chose to take care of himself, mostly by himself, so he could take the time to ponder what life is all about. In his day, and especially in our day, each of us is told from childhood that we must rush about all day long—get an education so you can get a job so you can occupy yourself all day with some mundane dollar-making activity so you can die in peace. Yes, perhaps it is not all that bad, but I can recall sitting through endless hours of "the job" and feeling so spiritually and mentally stifled, all the while telling myself I had no other choice. I realized from reading Thoreau that there are endless choices we can make to create the type of life we want to live. And there are many forms of work beside the job that you do for money.

I respect the courage that it took for Thoreau to build his own home, and produce his own food, and take the time to have meaningful conversations with the other denizens of the forest. And perhaps the most meaningful point that I derived from Thoreau, and other such seekers-of-meaning, is that you don't really have to go anywhere else, and you don't need to wait for someone or something. Just take one step to creating and living a "sustainable" lifestyle. Do it now, today, where you are. That was the lesson I learned from Thoreau, Marshall Greenwood, Richard E. White, and a handful of other pioneers I have met along the way.

THE MODERN WORLD

In my quest for sustainability, voluntary simplicity, and ecological living, I am well aware that the technological aspects of our world have changed dramatically, in some cases year by year. We now have interconnectedness via the internet, and apps, and smartphones, and wireless, and drones, and instant gratification in almost all areas. These are all mixed blessings, since they provide us with so many benefits, yet at the same time, we are increasingly dependent on these new technologies to get our information and our supplies. We thus live in an increasingly more dangerous world, since the ground-level knowledge of how to do the most basic skills of human life is less and less commonplace.

Regardless of all the technologies you decide to use, never lose sight of the fact that any electronic conveyance can fail you when you least expect it, for reasons way beyond your control. Never lose sight of the fact that your skills that you have worked hard to develop are always yours, and your relationships with other people (especially in hard times) are more valuable than gold.

I hope that you find this book useful in your quest for self-reliance. This is a very basic blueprint of what anyone can do in their own home, in their own yards, to be a part of the solution to the ecological crisis facing us all. It should be clear to you that each chapter of this slim book could be an entire book. My goal, however, was to provide the basic overview of what each of you can do now. We welcome your suggestions and questions.

CHAPTER ONE

THE CITY: IS THERE AN IDEAL FORM?

"The measure of any great civilization is its cities and a measure of a city's greatness is to be found in the quality of its public spaces, its parks and squares."—*John Ruskin*

WHAT IS A LIVEABLE CITY? A SUSTAINABLE VIEW OF PUBLIC SPACES...

As populations inevitably increase, and urban centers grow more crowded, how *should* we think about the public spaces that everyone uses? Let's talk a little about *public* spaces before we get to your personal space.

The public spaces in our cities can define how we feel, and what we do. They can define the very nature of our existence, much in the way that geography nearly always defines the character and the activities of the people who live there. How we build out our public spaces can create a fulfilling and exciting life, or it can lead to hell on Earth. While it is probably not possible to create public spaces for large numbers of people that please all the people all the time, we can still attempt to define the ideal public spaces in terms of human scale, sustainability, ecologic principles, health, and enjoyability.

The economics involved in planning, permitting, and building public spaces are obvious aspects that can prove to be limiting factors, in some cases. Sometimes, money is not a limitation, per se, but rather a motivating factor. If there is much more money to be made by adding ever-more buildings than there is in creating, or preserving, open and/or green space, the monetary side all too often wins. Yes, it often comes down to just that: profit now vs. long-term sustainability, one of the huge realities that face those who fight for sustainable public spaces, especially where private property, and personal profits, are involved—as they often are.

THE MEXICAN ZOCALO

I decided to live in Cuernavaca, Mexico, one summer some years ago, for the express purpose of learning Spanish. During this first long stay in Mexico, I experienced a mindset that governs life and the ways that their towns and cities are used. Indeed, "public space" was a concept that was very real and alive in this town, and in nearly all the small towns I visited in Mexico.

Like the town square of every small American town, every Mexican town has at least one zocalo. The zocalo is the large square where there is typically a raised platform for speakers and music. There are large paved areas for walking, or dancing. The zocalo is often arranged with rows of trees throughout, and nearly always with a perimeter of trees. Many of the Mexican zocalos have rows of stores on all four sides. On the weekends, there are often musical events, and temporary booths that would appear for craft and food vendors to provide for the many shoppers. The zocalo is the place to meet people. You feel safe and comfortable there.

I realized that the zocalo was not so much the product of a city engineer as it was the organic manifestation of a society that likes to meet together, and insists on having that place to do so. The zocalo probably has its roots in the large central ball courts of the Maya and Aztecs, which appeared to be the center of social, political, and religious life. Every town and city needs its zocalo—perhaps with some tweaks—as the most ecological way to let our building practices support a healthy population.

The Mexican zocalo is heavily planted, and full of benches to sit. It is a place where crafters sell their products and musicians play.

Entertainers attract a crowd in a Mexican zocalo.

When one sees the vastness of the ball courts and other open spaces of the Maya, you wonder how exactly these spaces were used. Were these the precursors to the zocalo and town square?

A LESSON NOT ALWAYS LEARNED

As I have traveled through many cities of southern California, and throughout the United States, I realize that every community needs public space, and the zocalo or traditional public square is a great place to start. It must be centrally located, and it must be inviting. It must be where people will naturally go, and it must feel safe. It need not be massive—many of the world's great public spaces are relatively small. A great view of a lake or ocean is nice, but not essential. It has to be people-friendly where you can sit and meet your neighbors, get a bite to eat, and feel confident to say hello to anyone present.

Of course, there are many attempts to create great new public spaces, but sometimes the priorities are not in order. There are many examples of *commercial* public space in the United States, which can be an open or enclosed mall, or other shopping sites where they have placed a token fountain and statue and some grass so you don't feel that it is *entirely* for commercial purposes. Except that, it is.

GENERAL ECOLOGIC PRINCIPLES FOR PUBLIC SPACE

What are the basic principles that should govern the thinking of urban planners and architects when planning meaningful public space? I may not automatically define these factors as I walk through various public spaces, but I will inevitably be left with some impression—which can range from feeling very uplifted, to the other extreme of wanting to get out of there as quickly as possible.

So, when urban planners examine great public spaces, certain aspects are most commonly cited for that "greatness" that we all want to experience.

PEOPLE-FRIENDLY

The space need not be prohibitively large, like the great Russian plazas where thousands of soldiers neatly line up when the weapons are promenaded each year in front of the politburo. Such a vast expanse of cement is not people-friendly. A good public space feels good, looks good, and smells good (food and flowering trees). People want to be there. It is most likely a place where vehicles are not allowed, though this is not always the case.

Local merchants sell homemade products in this Mexican zocalo, or town square.

FLORA

Lawns are not essential, but green spaces are necessary. If it's absolutely not possible to have pockets or lines of fragrant and beautiful vegetation, there should at least be as many trees as possible. Trees should be selected that are appropriate to the area, and planners need to do their homework and discover which local native plants would do best in a public space. Yes, trees that produce food would be great, but you'd not want to plant fruit or nut trees that require an excessive amount of cleanup, or that would attract rats or ants.

Farmers markets allow people to buy fresh produce, and meet their neighbors. They do not require large amounts of space, but should be inviting and attractive.

The public space should offer a balance of nature, commerce, culture, and community.

Oscar Duardo operates a neighborhood public garden in northeast Los Angeles, on an old house lot, immediately adjacent to the downtown district.

Neighborhood gardens often co-exist in the urban downtown areas, where they are perhaps needed the most.

In what had been a large cement sprawl, the city of Pasadena ha "softened" the area by planting drought-tolerant plants around much of the perimeter.

Guerilla gardeners will plant corn and other plants wherever there is bare soil.

Rooftop trees and plants can add shade, oxygen, and beauty to downtown areas.

WATER WORKS

Some great public spaces are near lakes, or rivers, or an ocean. People are always attracted to water because it feels good to be around water, and the negative ions around water make such spots healthy places to be. If a public space is not around water, it would be good to add a pond or a fountain. To keep the water circulated, solar-powered pumps are relatively easy to obtain these days.

A public water fountain. Where water is scarce, it can be recycled.

A popular and traditional fountain at Pasadena's city hall.

CHAIRS AND BENCHES

People stand and people walk, and in the places where we gather, we sit. A great public space really needs chairs and tables, ideally built

A water feature in a shopping venue which mimics a stream and small waterfall.

locally of cement so they last forever, or built from local wood by local craftspeople. Still, there are public spaces with no chairs or tables, and they are inviting places where you can even sit on the ground as you wish.

ARTWORK

Artwork is not essential to a public space, though the buildings and infrastructure can easily contain art in the form of sculpture or murals.

Planners of public spaces should always think long term, and avoid current fads or movements. Avoid political or religious themes in public art, and avoid extreme abstracts that invite derision or confusion. I have a personal bias toward art that is realistic and meaningful. For example, the Protection statue at Forest Lawn mortuary in Glendale, California, is one of my favorites.

THE NATURAL LANDSCAPE

Because so many urban public places have been created from the ground up, they may look "natural," though they are not. Those which

Universal themes are best. Here is the famous "Protection" statue, where the father holds the bow, protecting the mother with child.

Here Pasadena honors its famous son, Jackie Robinson, in the city hall square.

Public art in Tabasco, Mexico, featuring the enigmatic "Olmec heads," whose identity remains a mystery. These were dug out of the ground, remnants of the pre-Mayan culture, and are now popular public art, embodying art and culture.

Unique metal musicians in Yucatan.

do the best are those where the planners took careful note of the actual pre-existing landscape. They took into account the wind flow for that area, the movement of sun and shade throughout the day, the contours of the land. And they chose plants and trees which in time become an integral part of that landscape. If edible plants are grown, such as fruit trees, it's best to get a local organization on board first, such as an organization that would make sure all the fruit is collected, and used, and not left to rot and become a problem.

THE JAPAN MODEL

Remember, "public space" is not simply the public square. Public space is any space that is not privately owned, and over which the local jurisdiction can exercise some control. In some cases, what we call "public space" can also be applied to the private space that we see, referring to such cases where billboards on private land can still mar an otherwise beautiful view that you experience while walking or driving on public land. This can also refer to a tall building that blocks your view of the mountains, or a tall building that blocks out your sunlight.

It is worth looking at the Japanese model.

THE DESIGN CODE

What is loosely called the "design code" in Manazuru, Kanagawa, Japan, gradually developed because the residents loved the quality of their city. Because those special qualities attracted ever-more people who wanted to reside there, business interests were also attracted. The local people created a series of concepts to maintain the character of the city, the character that attracted everyone there in the first place.

The design code is similar to the building and safety codes of major cities, but rather than strict rules, it is more a series of overall guidelines. Builders would meet with local legislators and other citizens to make sure their project meets the design code. In some cases, the project is disallowed. In some cases, the project will be modified so that the spirit of the design code is maintained. Briefly, here are some of the key elements of the design code.

DON'T BLOCK THE VIEW OF THE OCEAN

In many US and European cities, land rights are regarded as vertical, and land owners are often allowed whatever meets building guidelines and height guidelines. Blocking your neighbor's view is typically not regarded. However, in Manazuru, everyone's view is regarded as important. In planning meetings, the effect of your project on the neighbor's view would be discussed. The view of the ocean is so special to everyone that new buildings and additions must not obscure your neighbor's view.

PASSAGEWAYS AND ALLEYS BETWEEN HOUSES

One of the quaint features of Manazuru and surrounding areas is the alleyways that run between the houses. These are narrow paths, not full streets, and they allow walkers to get around, and often meet their neighbors. Maintaining these walkways is an integral part of the design code. It also means that houses will not be built right atop each other, as you see done in parts of San Francisco and other big cities in the US.

KEEP ALL THE CITRUS TREES

Citrus trees were once widely planted throughout Kanagawa, and they are regarded as a local treasure. Thus, residents are urged to not cut any of them down, and even to plant more. They are regarded not just as a source of food for the body, but as a source of food for the soul as well.

LOCALLY SOURCE BUILDING SUPPLIES

Where possible, the design code encourages builders and homeowners to use local timber and stone and other local building materials. Not only does this provide somewhat of a consistent appearance, but it is also beneficial in that it seeks to continually support local craftspeople.

WORK WITH NEIGHBORS TO GET AGREEMENTS

One of the key elements of the design code is that it requires builders to not hide what they are planning, but to openly discuss it with those whom the project may affect. This takes time, and is not always easy. However, when both "sides" meet together, face to face, and share their concerns, most of the obstacles and challenges can be resolved equitably.

Of course, the design code is not a panacea, and may not be as easy to institute in countries that do not have the group ethic that you find in Japan. Still, city planners whose blueprints and ideas shape the feel of public space should seriously study the design code.

SUMMARY

For a public space to be noteworthy and special, the following qualities should all be present:

- The space is safe and welcoming to all who live nearby. People should not only want to visit such a place, but they should want to return often.
- There must be space where people can walk or bicycle, where automobiles are not present.
- The local culture and history should be reflected in some way (e.g., Olvera Street in old downtown Los Angeles).
- There are social activities that occur there that invite people to enter (e.g., food, dance, meetings, chess, music, Tai Chi, etc.).
- There are architectural or natural features that are appealing and of interest to all ages.
- The public space must have a good relationship to the surrounding area, whether that is stores, or schools, or park spaces. The best public places are surrounded by diversity, not uniformity.
- The space must be well maintained, and kept clean. This may mean hiring a maintenance staff, or organizing volunteers. Good public spaces can be quickly abandoned by most people if they fill with trash and graffiti, and criminal activity.

A great public space should have as many of these qualities as possible. The designers of the space (especially where it was designed from the ground up) must also grasp that the space will be entered and used by living, breathing people who live in that area. A great public space is not a static museum to be looked at, but it is rather a dynamic entity, vitalistic, which (if properly conceived) will take on a life of its own, and will serve to uplift all who go there.

CHAPTER TWO

SHELTER: OUR PERSONAL LIVING SPACES

Now that we've discussed the "big picture," let's look at our personal living spaces. If you're living in the city, you're living in a house or apartment. You own your place, or you rent a place. This book is addressed to the average urban dweller who enjoys the benefits of urban living, but dislikes what seems to be the inherent overuse and misuse of resources that city living seems to encourage and accept. Most city dwellers don't think about it too much, but too many of the urban resources are provided from outside agencies, such as electricity, plumbing for our water, and natural gas.

Our goal is to make your home—even a small urban home—more ecological and sustainable. You probably can't be a fully self-sufficient farmer, but you can grow at least some of your food. You can use your garbage to create soil. You can use fewer electrical appliances and decrease your dependence, and you can use more manual appliances. You can learn to capture some of the sun that shines on your home for electricity and cooking your food. You can begin to capture some of the rain that falls on your place, and you can do your best to keep all your rain on your property. In other words, you can maximize the ecological quotient of your little place in the city. You can be a part of the solution.

In this chapter, let's discuss how you can make the shelter you live in more economical and ecological.

Let's look at the many time-proven methods that you can do so that your home will provide you with warmth in the summer, and cooling in the winter, simply by the way the house is built, modified, and located.

[Note: This book does not address building an efficient home from the ground up. That sort of information can be found in countless other books, such as Living Homes: Stone Masonry, Log and Strawbale Construction, 6th Edition, 2010, by Tom Elpel, *or* The New Net Zero: Leading-Edge Design and Construction of Homes and Buildings for a Renewable Energy Future (2014), by Bill Maclay, *and other books.]*

DEALING WITH HEAT AND COLD
HOW TO BE COOL

There are natural forces that we can tap in order to stay cooler indoors when it is scorching hot outside. Part of our ability to tap these natural forces has much to do with how well the house was planned, and aligned in its particular terrain, and how well it was built. Unfortunately for most of us, we're living in a house built by someone decades ago with no regard to sun and wind alignment, and no regard to ecological and economical living. So we end up trying to do the best we can with what we have. We have to find the way to make the best of a bad situation. So let's try to get back to the basics. Let's review some of the many principles that enable us to stay cool.

We are always assaulted by the forces of nature, especially in the form of what we call weather—heat, cold, wind, rain, storms. How the masses of hot air and cold air come together and create weather is fascinating, and you'd benefit by learning more about it in a good book such as Eric Sloane's *Weather Book*.

Part of the problem of settled people is that we have plopped ourselves down in our homes and cities and we have no desire nor ability to move nomadically with the seasons. Plus, there are just too many of us today to do that. So we deal with the conditions of weather, wherever we are.

Before we address specific details of your house, let's just take a moment and look at our own body and how it's designed to help us stay cool.

When it's hot, we sweat. The sweat cools us down a bit. Yet in our modern world, people are often inappropriately concerned about the fact that our bodies are designed to sweat. There is a million-dollar industry designed to make us smell good because we sweat. I understand that. But any drugs or surgery designed to prevent the body from sweating is *not* a good idea, and ultimately bad for the health of the body. The body is designed to sweat for a reason. The pores not only excrete water to help cool us down, but they also excrete toxins.

LIQUIDS

As we sweat, we are losing water in the process. So when it's hot, we should also drink more fluids. Now, we drink to replenish fluids, but some fluids actually lead to a greater net loss than a net gain. For example, alcohol, and sometimes coffee, might replenish the water our body is losing by sweating, but the increase in perspiration and urination may be greater than what we're putting in. So, when it is very hot, drink more fluids, but not alcohol.

Research has shown that by adding a little bit of raw apple cider vinegar to our drinking water or fruit juice will enable us to deal with the heat just a little better.

During the late 1970s, when I first learned of this through the WTI Survival Training School, I would routinely add from one teaspoon to one tablespoon of raw apple cider vinegar to each quart of drinking water (or fruit juice). After working in the heat, I found that I was far less exhausted when I'd added the vinegar to the water than when I did not. I have experienced this enough times to know that it was not merely psychosomatic. Plus, I have experienced the added bonus of having mosquitoes leave me alone when they are biting everyone else. Apparently, the vinegar does something to my body chemistry or blood which causes the mosquitoes to find me undesirable, which is good.

Wilderness Guide Ed Parker shows raw apple cider vinegar.

CLOTHING

Next, during times of heat, adjust your clothing accordingly. This should be easy enough to do when at home, and you ought to have a wardrobe for both summer and winter. Summer clothes should be of lighter fabric, and cotton and natural fabrics are best. Polyesters do not "breathe" as well as cottons. They should not be too tight, but should fit loosely.

Have you ever seen how the people dress who live their lives in the desert? They wear loose-fitting robes! Note how different that is from the average American who gets a free weekend and travels to the desert to look at wildflowers or to the beach, wearing the skimpiest of outfits. This is perhaps fine if you want to show off, and good for peeping Tom photographers, but not great for your body's health.

Once, while leading a group on a wilderness class in the heat of the summer, two hikers came dressed in shorts and tank tops. The woman says to me, "Why are you dressed like that?" I was wearing long khaki pants, a light cotton khaki shirt, and a wide-brimmed hat. I was very comfortable and wanted to stay that way. Before I could answer, they ambled off into the wild blue yonder.

Later in the day, as I was still hydrated and feeling good, they passed us again as they were coming back, heading up the hill to their car. They looked tired, haggard, dragging their feet. Their skin was brilliant pink. "Do any of you know what poison oak looks like?" she asked, but didn't wait around as we attempted to answer, simply continuing on the trail, dragging their feet and kicking up dust.

"Do you see what I see?" I asked my students. We then had a brief discussion about how the hiking couple went into the heat overexposed and lost moisture, got scratched up and sun-burned, and were probably close to heat stroke. With their short pants, they probably walked through the ubiquitous poison oak. My long pants and shirt, loose-fitting and of light fabric, protected me from all that. Additionally, as it was a very hot day, my students and I would occasionally wet our clothes from the little stream and let our clothes be our "swamp cooler" that we were wearing.

DIET

Diet is also something you should keep in mind when it is very hot. Heavy starchy food requires more water for your body to digest and assimilate, and is best avoided. Salads, fruits, fruit drinks, vegetables, and lighter foods cause less stress to your body in times of heat. It is no great mystery that watermelon is a favorite food in summer.

There are adjustments that you can make to your diet and clothing to render your body less vulnerable to the heat.

SIX SIMPLE WAYS TO KEEP THE BODY COOL

TECHNIQUE	REASON
Stay out of the sun if possible.	Obvious, no?
Drink fluids regularly.	Loss of water through perspiration renders our body less able to cool itself.
Don't eat heavy, starchy foods.	These foods require more water to digest.
Wear a hat with a broad brim.	The hat protects your face from sunburn and water loss.
Wear loose clothing.	Tight clothing constricts, and offers minimal insulation from the heat.
Wear long pants, long-sleeved shirt, long dress when in the sun.	Protect your body from the drying effects of the sun.

Now let's get to your house and yard.

Let's first assume that you did not build your home, aligning it so that you get the best solar exposure in winter, and the least in summer, with trees and landscaping to take advantage of the local geology and wind flow. Let's assume you are like 95 percent of the people who live in cities who simply purchased or rented a place and now have to make the best of the situation. I have been in that situation numerous times. Sometimes the house was ideally suited to taking advantage of nature's forces, and sometimes not.

In my Highland Park home, it was beastly hot every summer. The house was built in a low pocket in a valley, and there seemed to be no wind flow through the area. It was not ideally suited to take advantage of the sun in the winter, nor was it ideally suited to take advantage of natural cooling in the summer. Here are some of the things we did, little by little.

Out of desperation one summer, we went to Sears and purchased a window air conditioner. We knew nothing about the Energy Star program; we simply purchased an air conditioner that we could afford. This appliance worked really well at keeping the house temperature tolerable during those ten to twenty days a year when it was unbearable. But it sucked up electricity and drove up the bill, something we didn't like.

WHITE ROOF

At this same time, our roof was no good and we needed a new one. I knew that sooner or later we'd need to bite the bullet and reroof the entire place. But—my natural instinct being to save the money and to put off the roofing project as long as possible—I found a short-term alternative, which was a white liquid rubber product that I painted over the existing roof like thick paint. (There are several such products at home improvement stores; the last one I purchased was called Henry's Solarflex 287.)

A white roof keeps the house cool.

Another white roof that keeps the house cool.

Remember, my primary intent was to seal all the leaks in a bad roof until I could afford to hire roofers. I wasn't happy that the product was brilliant white since I assumed that my roof would be a brilliant beacon to every plane and helicopter for twenty miles in all directions. But then I learned that, besides sealing small leaks, this product was also marketed to folks who live in trailers and mobile homes, and folks with metal roofs that get hot. Once the roof was sealed in this white rubber product, we found that the inside temperature during the heat of summer was about 15°F cooler. This was a significant difference, and it meant that the air conditioner was now on maybe three or four days a year, not ten to twenty.

I have used this white rubber product on the roof of every house I have lived in since then, and found that the inside temperature during the day stays at least 15°F cooler, all a result of the reflective qualities of white. I would strongly recommend this product to anyone, and when reroofing, always insist on the whitest possible shingles.

ATTIC SPACE

Once when my friend Eric Zammit was visiting, we got to talking about natural methods of cooling one's home. I told him that I wanted to insulate my attic but had not yet done so because I was thinking of tearing out the ceiling and creating a much larger inside space. Eric pointed out that he had a similar problem in his home, and that I would be better off not taking out my ceiling. Even without insulation, Eric said, that space between the ceiling and the roof traps heat and actually serves as a buffer to keep the house cooler. So I never removed the ceilings.

INSULATION

In fact, probably the most cost-effective single thing that a homeowner could do to be cooler in summer (and warmer in winter) is to heavily insulate every wall in the house, as well as the ceiling and the floor space. Regardless of what method you then use to cool (or heat) your home, your heavy insulation will then keep the house cool in summer and warm in winter.

There are lots of ways to insulate walls and wall spaces, even with foam that can be blown in via a little hole so you don't need to rip out the walls in order to insulate. Obviously, it would have been better if this was done as the house was being built, but if it wasn't, you can still insulate little by little as you can afford it, beginning with the rooms that you use the most, or that you want to keep the coolest (or warmest).

This is one of those projects that costs more now, but pays off in the long run with lower bills.

Part of the insulation process is to get double-walled windows, meaning windows that contain at least two panes of glass, providing an insulating air pocket between the two glass layers, thus cutting down on heat or cold loss by means of conduction and convection.

So before you get all excited about installing solar panels to operate your inefficient cooling system, slow down, and do first things first. The best bang for your buck will come with insulating everything— walls, attic, floor space. An insulated house will stay cooler in summer and warmer in winter.

In some climates, heavy insulation could mean that you could reduce your use of a cooler or heater, or entirely eliminate the need to purchase a costly air conditioner or heating system.

ATTIC FAN

After talking with Eric Zammitt, I went up into the attic on a hot day and realized it was VERY hot up there—maybe 20°F hotter in the attic space than it was down in the living room. Of course, that is partly because heat rises, but also because the sun was beating down on the roof. What else could we do that wouldn't cost an arm and a leg to make the inside of the house cooler?

I had solar installer Wade Webb come over and look at a used solar panel that I had in my garage. Wade had previously installed our small solar electric system. I showed Wade the solar panel, whose surface was cracked; I had picked it out of a trash can where someone had tossed it. Wade tested it and found that it was still able to generate electricity. I epoxied a clear plastic sheet over the top surface so no water would get inside, and then Wade worked another miracle on the roof. He installed a small 12-volt fan in the attic at one of the existing attic vents, and then wired the fan to the refurbished solar panel. He then attached an on/off switch that was installed in a closet, which allowed us to turn on the fan during the summer when it was hot, but leave it off in the winter. By using the power of the sun, we were able to blow the heat out of the attic, dropping the attic heat by many degrees, and making the house much more comfortable and livable during the summer.

There are also numerous commercial sun-powered attic fans to look into. One is the SolarStar attic fan, a one-piece unit with a fan to suck the hot air out of your attic, with a solar module on top to power it. This unit does not have an on-off switch; instead, it works whenever there is sun striking the module. It is simple, and easy for the homeowner to install.

A view of the fan of this simple rooftop mounted solar fan.

An example of a commercially available solar roof fan. The electricity is generated by the photo-voltaics on the top.

It's a never-ending task to keep track of all the latest products that help the consumer save energy, so I suggest you talk to someone in a home improvement store, or online, and study the energy-saving products that are available.

Keep in mind that each of these measures helped just a little, and they were starting to add up.

Could we get things any cooler using just natural principles?

AIR CIRCULATION

One of the problems with this particular house was that it was set in a low spot with little air circulation. And the inside of the house was very hot during the summer, even at night.

We knew that we would have better air circulation by opening certain windows, which we did, and that helped to a certain extent. But the north to south air flow was blocked by the rear and front doors, and we were hesitant to leave the doors open all night with just flimsy screen doors for protection. Remember, this was Los Angeles. Yes, it is good to trust one's neighbors, but anyone could be passing through in the night in L.A., and so we installed some iron security screen doors on the front and rear. This allowed us to keep the front and rear doors open all night, and get the air flow that kept the temperature very comfortable and never muggy and stuffy. Plus, we now felt that we didn't have to worry every minute that we might have to rush for a gun if we heard some intruder suddenly entering.

Once you've performed all these low-tech measures, you'll find that they all add up. And before you go out and buy an energy-efficient Energy Star–rated cooler, let's look at just a few more possibilities.

AIR FLOW

Once, while visiting Mr. White (the founder of the non-profit "survival" think tank) in his Highland Park home on a hot summer day, I noted that there was no air conditioning or even a fan, and certainly no "central air." It was a 140-year-old house, built before electricity was the norm. It was not cold or even "cool" in their living room, as is often the case when you enter modern stores and offices in summer. But, it was definitely comfortable, and far cooler than the stifling 100°F+ heat outside. What had he done?

The living room was a large, approximately twenty-five- by ten-foot room, with the long side facing south with two large windows. There was a door on the east and a window on the west. The large picture windows were covered with sheets. This still allowed in light, but kept out much of the brightness and heat of the sun. Both the east door and the west window were open, and both were covered in a wet sheet, which was periodically replaced with another wet one. (As I recall, they put some newspaper underneath where some water dripped.) There was a cool air breeze through the room and the air was cooled by the moisture in the sheets. In essence, we weren't all sitting in a living room, but in a giant "swamp cooler."

It turns out that ancient Egyptians invented the first swamp coolers when they hung camel hair rugs, soaked in water, over the doorways and windows of their living spaces, precisely as White had done in his own home.

Air flow is important, and you should make a point of observing your local air flows.

I have cooled my home at night simply with open doors—a no-brainer. But some houses have a more-complicated air-flow pattern, so you need to take the time to observe the patterns in your home.

HEAT RISES

One way that I've observed to keep a large two-story house cooler in summer involved opening the windows on the northern shady side, and the cooler shaded (by trees) east side, and opening one upper window just a crack in the upstairs west side. Picture, if you will, the hot air rising in the house, flowing out that western crack, but bringing with it a slight air flow of the cooler air from the cooler side of the house. This may seem like a little thing, but it is one of the many little things that enable you to live in relative comfort without using any resources. It allows you to live with nature's principles.

Coincidentally, Native Americans of the Plains, during the days when tipis dominated the flatlands, also utilized natural air flow. On very hot days on the Plains, the bottom part of the tipi canvas would be rolled up a foot or so, to leave an open space all around the bottom. Hot air rising in a narrower space (such as in the cone shape of the tipi) will speed up just slightly as the air exits the smoke flap. This is known as the Venturi effect, and allowed Native Americans to have a type of air conditioning without electricity.

[The "Venturi effect" is named after its discoverer, Giovanni Battista Venturi, who noted the reduction in fluid pressure that results when a fluid flows through a constricted section (or choke) of a pipe. In fluid dynamics, an incompressible fluid's velocity increases as it passes through a constriction. This same principle can be observed in the motion of air.]

There are still more simple ways that people have used to cut down the heat in their home. Simple, but not always easy to implement.

For example, if you live in the desert, your home is assaulted by the heat all the time. Trees help, and a white roof helps, but some enterprising desert dwellers have built what amounts to a massive canopy over their home. In the ones that I have seen, such as at the farm of Joe Avitua near Visalia, California, large vertical posts had been secured around the house, and a "roof" of sheet metal was installed. This created a buffer between the heat of the sun and the roof of the house. This is akin to the attic space in the house that provides some insulating space, therefore keeping the home cooler.

Another large-scale innovation, also done on desert homes, was to create a large flat roof, over which canvas was secured. Water is then run down over the roof from the top, and is absorbed by the fabric before it is evaporated. In essence, this method is like having a large swamp cooler over your home. I don't know if anyone is still building such roofs in their desert homes, but it has been documented on Hugh Howser's public television programs.

FORBES' ADVICE

I spoke to Glenn Forbes, who manages to produce all of his own energy needs in Sylmar, California, with a unique wind generator and a few dozen solar panels. He shared some common-sense suggestions for natural cooling and heating.

He told me, "If you are expecting hot days, open the windows all night long to remove any heat buildup. Do the reverse for heating. Shade trees around your home are good too. Also consider misters to cool things off. If the humidity is low, swamp coolers are good."

One of the objections that many folks have to opening the windows at night is fear of intruders. Indeed, many robbers and rapists have gained access to homes when the windows were open. Before I moved into my Altadena home, all the windows had security bars, and there were security screen doors. The owner of the place offered to remove them, thinking that I would find them unsightly. "Leave them there," I told him, and this has allowed me to keep doors and windows open day and night, as needed, and not worry about various wild barbarians invading my home. Plus, everyone in the neighborhood knew that I had a pitbull, and though he was the sweetest dog ever, it probably deterred more than one would-be burglar.

STEVE LAMB'S ADVICE

I talked with Steve Lamb, Altadena resident and architect, about how to increase the cooling and heating efficiency of our homes.

According to Lamb, "The first and perhaps most important thing you can do to make a house naturally energy efficient is to properly site the home. You want natural early morning light from high windows in the bedrooms, meaning you want your bedrooms on the east. You want most of your solar heat gain from the south, and you want to reduce your western late afternoon heat gain in the summer, but use it in the winter by planting deciduous trees that drop leaves in winter but shade in summer. Shading your bedroom with trees during the summer is also a smart thing to do. My 1906 single-wall (one-inch-thick redwood walls) house follows these strategies and it is comfortable year-round.

"In the southern California climate, you want as much cooling shading roof overhang as you can get," he continued. "If you think three feet is good, go to five feet. This creates a cooler micro-climate around the house and keeps your wall areas from heating up. You can do what Frank Lloyd Wright did and open the rafters at the points where you want solar heat gain.

The famous Gamble House with the deep overhangs for shade.

Architect Steve Lamb next to a modest home to which he added the overhang to create more shade.

Lamb had some key points to make on how to plan efficiency into a building:

SIZE

"Most people think they need too many rooms," says Lamb, "and that they need them too big. I have been in some gigantic homes that were no more comfortable or expansive to the mind than a shoebox. I have seen small homes with well-planned vistas and a sense of openness that made you feel you were in the most open expansive place imaginable.

"A 12x24x8 room is 2,128 cubic feet to heat and cool. A room with the same or even lower function that is 16x36x12 is 6,876 cubic feet to heat and cool. It's double the square feet, but triple the cubic feet. Worse yet, the larger the mass of air to heat and cool, the more difficult it is to heat and cool it and the more difficult it is to keep it at temperature, and the more important the air leaks become. So whatever you can do to reduce the volume of the rooms and keep open sight lines for the psychological benefit of the inhabitants is vital. The worst thing you can is make a tall vertical room. That's like just throwing heating and cooling money down the sewer. The more horizontal a room, the more its tendency to transfer the warm or cool air across to the inhabitants. The more vertical, the more the tendency to transfer the hot or cool air up and out and away from the inhabitants. Vertical rooms also can lead to inversion layers where the hot air rises and forces the cool air down, not desirable in winter.

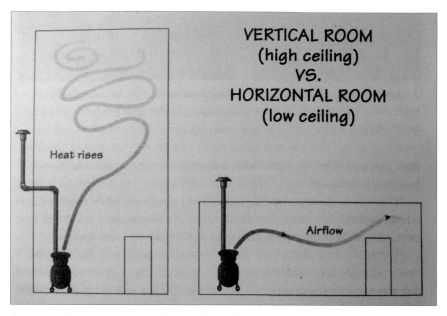

VERTICAL ROOM
(high ceiling)
VS.
HORIZONTAL ROOM
(low ceiling)

Heat rises

Airflow

"The more horizontal a room, the more its tendency to transfer the warm or cool air across to the inhabitants. The more vertical, the more the tendency to transfer the warm or cool air up and away from the inhabitants. Vertical rooms can lead to inversion layers where the hot air rises and forces the cool air down, which is not desirable in winter." – Steve Lamb

"Having said that, high, well-insulated windows that are under the eaves and don't really have views are excellent devices for taking heat off the ceiling in the summer and causing drafts for cooling. You could make some out of plywood and cork sandwich, cork being the best natural insulator, but nowadays the code requires any hinged opening device to be made by an approved manufacturer, so until someone starts making them in a factory, we are stuck with the less-efficient windows.

"None of these ideas is new. They were common folk knowledge, and they were found in the work by some arts and crafts architects such as Frank Lloyd Wright, early Greene & Greenes, all of Louis B. Easton's work, and even by Richard Neutra in his work before WW2.

"A book that has some of the best ideas in it and that is still ahead of the times in what it demonstrates as being available options is *Shelter*, by Ten Speed Press in Berkley, first published in the 1970s. Many of the ideas in there are still just as useful, practical, and more time-proven than ever, but still not allowed under our codes, even as the codes become more allegedly 'green.'"

AIR CONDITIONING SYSTEMS

The Real Goods *Solar Living Source Book*—an excellent all-around reference for all the products you need for self-reliant living—gives some common-sense advice on how to reduce costs with a conventional air conditioning system. For example, simply keeping the unit checked and maintained on a regular basis will ensure maximum efficiency and longevity. They recommend a programmable thermostat, and recommend that you turn off your air conditioning if you're leaving home for more than an hour. Also clean that filter at least every month when you're using the air conditioner.

SWAMP COOLERS

Swamp coolers, also known as evaporative coolers, work best in the Southwest where humidity is low. The lower the humidity, the better these work. In the right location, a swamp cooler can save you up to 50 percent of the initial cost, and up to 80 percent of operating costs. These work by drawing fresh outside air through wet porous pads, and blowing the cooler air into the room.

HEAT PUMPS

Heat pumps can be used for both heating and cooling. They work by extracting warmth and coolness from the outside air or ground. According to the August 2008 issue of *Scientific American*, "heat pumps can provide greater efficiency and lower cost over the long haul … They can attain greater efficiency than conventional designs because instead of consuming fuel to generate warmth or coolness from scratch, they exploit heat or cold already present in the outside air or ground."

They move this heat or cold around via electricity, so they are thus considered the most efficient form of electric heat. These are essentially air conditioners with a switch so they can be used for either cooling or heating. These are considered best in climates with colder winters, or where natural gas is not available.

One air conditioning service man I spoke to said that the initial cost is more, and that though they are more efficient over time, they do not heat as well as gas furnaces. This was his explanation as to why heat pumps are still only a small proportion of the air conditioning market.

SEVEN SIMPLE WAYS TO KEEP THE HOUSE COOL (there are many more!)

MEASURE	WHAT IT DOES	COST	DIU? Rated 1 to 5 (1 is easiest)
Coat the roof white	Reflects the heat	Approx. $200 for average roof	1
Deep awnings over windows	Keeps the sun out	Built into cost of house construction	3
Allow cooling air flow	Cools your house naturally	A factor of proper house siting	N/A
Keep doors open at night (use security doors)	Allows cool air through house	Approx. $100 a door	2
Solar attic fan	Sucks hot air out of attic	Approx. $200	3
Swamp cooler	Brings cooler outside air inside	Approx. $100	1
Insulation in walls, ceiling, floors	Keeps the cold in, and, in winter, keeps the warmth in	Varies significantly	3 to 4

QUIZ:

1. What is the Venturi Effect? [see page 29]
2. What measure (discussed above) gives you the biggest "bang for your buck"?

ANSWER:

1. In the case of Plains Indians' tipis, air flowing upward inside the tipi is constricted at the top exit, causing an increased speed of air flow. It was regarded as natural form of "air conditioning."
2. Insulating the ceiling, walls, and floors.

HOW TO STAY WARM

Some of the principles of keeping your place warm when it's cold outside have already been addressed. But let's start from the beginning. Let's start with you and what you do and what you wear. Then we'll get to the more mundane issues of how to keep your place warmer when it's freezing outside.

We're all different, with different likes and dislikes, and different tolerances to temperature variations. Up to a point, I like the cold. I like the doors open and the windows wide open, especially when it's raining outside. I like the feel of the breeze and the coolness of the air. There is something mentally and spiritually refreshing when the sweet rains and the cool breezes pass through my room.

But, how many times I have heard others say, "Can you please close the door, I'm freezing." Sometimes they say it politely, and sometime with anger.

I have my limits, of course. When I lived in Ohio with my brother, the winter temperature was once below zero for weeks. We had an oil furnace then, and it was expensive to heat the farmhouse without a woodstove, and so we blocked off the other rooms of the house and just heated the kitchen and bedroom, heating the living room only on occasion. One sunny winter day, the temperatures got "up to" 40°F and people in the town square were walking around in T-shirts, saying there's a heat wave. I was still in my coat, but it made it clear how our body's limitations are all very different.

Here in California, I don't get snow where I live and I enjoy the coldness and rain, which seem like pleasant gifts from God here in the desert environment of southern California.

Because of my state of mind, perhaps I deal with the cold better than I used to. But dealing with the cold is not merely a state of mind. There are practical things that can be done also.

For example, every pore of our body should be free of detritus and allow the body to excrete toxins. When clean, our pores are more able (within reason) to adjust our sense of comfort when it is hot or cold. So, to keep my pores doing their job, I thoroughly scrub my skin when I take baths, using a stiff brush that was probably designed to clean a sink or toilet.

I also drink warm fluids when it is very cold, despite the fact that this may mean that I go to the bathroom more often. This is so obvious that you wouldn't need to tell a child to have a warm beverage or hot soup on a cold day, but I know adults who won't drink hot tea or coffee (or even hot water) because they don't want to have to go to the bathroom more. In some very rare cases I can understand this, but usually, bathrooms are everywhere. We all have one in our homes, right? Consume warm beverages so you're more comfortable in the cold. A no-brainer.

Dress warmly. Another no-brainer.

Exercise a bit during the day. Another no-brainer. Obviously, any action that increases the cardio-vascular activity also warms us.

Upon hearing the above advice, someone once said to me, "You must be out of you mind! Should we be doing jumping jacks in the snow?!"

"That's not a bad idea," I thought, as he walked away.

Yes, I know this may not be for everyone, but simple lifestyle changes and modifications *can* make all the difference in the world.

After all, isn't it our very modern lifestyle that has created our ecological and economic crises in the first place? How long should we cling to the faulty logic of "I'm just doing what everyone else is doing" as the excuse to not change our behavior?

Okay, to the house.

In terms of the greatest energy savings per dollar spent ("the most bang for your buck"), insulating your walls, ceiling, and floor is by far the best investment. Before you concern yourself with exotic new appliances and fancy solar warmers, insulate!

LOW-TECH INSULATION

Fred Peters, a friend of my father who grew up in Bedford Heights, Ohio, often told the story of how he insulated his home. In Fred's neighborhood in the 1920s and '30s, everyone heated their homes with furnaces, and a truck would deliver the fuel when you needed it. In the winter, after snow had fallen, Fred noticed that the snow would always melt on the roofs of all the houses in his neighborhood. He reasoned that this was because all the heat from the furnace was being lost, and melting the snow.

Fred worked at a lumber mill at the time as an after-school job, and managed to bring home a bag of wood shavings every day in the following spring and summer. He took each bag and packed it into the attic spaces between the rafters. By the following winter, he'd fully insulated his attic by this method. He never told his father about it, since his father was a strict disciplinarian, and he felt his father would tell him not to do it.

As Fred came home each day the following winter, he began to notice that the snow on his family's house stayed longer than any other roof. He knew he was right, that by insulating his roof, he was keeping all the heat in the house.

Fred still hadn't told a thing to his father. A few weeks into the winter, Fred's dad told him that it must be a mild winter, because he noted that they still had plenty of fuel in the heater tank and hadn't needed to call the fuel delivery man as often.

Finally, Fred took his father outside and asked him to look at all the neighboring roofs, including their own. His father was mystified, and noticed for the first time that their roof was still full of snow while all the others were snow-free.

"What's going on?" said Fred's father. Fred then told his father what he'd done, how he'd gotten permission from work to bring home a bag or two of chips each day, and how he little by little filled all the gaps in the attic.

"And your father was delighted, right?" I asked Fred.

"My father hit the roof," said Fred. "I can't tell you how angry he was," Fred explained, pointing out the unfortunate fact that his father was mad because he was not in control. Still, within a week or so, Fred's father finally thanked and acknowledged him for the good thing he'd done.

I never forgot this story from my father's friend, and what he accomplished "in secret." Still, I wonder how fire-safe wood chips would be in the attic. Probably not very safe, and today's modern insulations are largely fire-retardant and would not represent the same potential fire danger, or weight, as wood chips in the attic.

MODERN APPLIANCES

ENERGY STAR

You might be ready to install another heating (or cooling) system. Do your homework before you make a purchase. Find out what is most appropriate for your needs.

Your best choice of an over-the-counter system will be those with the Energy Star "seal of approval." Energy Star is a joint program of the US Environmental Protection Agency and the US Department of Energy, "helping us all save money and protect the environment through energy-efficient products and practices," according to their website.

Rich Redman next to his Energy Star washing machine, which uses less water and power than other washing machines.

According to their website, "Results are already adding up. Americans, with the help of Energy Star, saved enough energy in 2007 alone to avoid greenhouse gas emissions equivalent to those from 27 million cars—all while saving $16 billion on their utility bills."

Choosing energy-efficient appliances can save families about a third on their energy bill with similar savings of greenhouse gas emissions, without sacrificing features, style, or comfort.

- If looking for new household products, look for ones that have earned the Energy Star. They meet strict energy efficiency guidelines set by the EPA and US Department of Energy.

- If looking for a new home, look for one that has earned the Energy Star.
- If looking to make larger improvements to your home, EPA offers tools and resources to help you plan and undertake projects to reduce your energy bills and improve home comfort.

FILTERS

In the central heating system in my father's house, there was a filter that had to be regularly cleaned and/or replaced. During the winter, my father would be in the basement regularly, shaking out the filter, or putting in a new one. This was a simple enough task, and as a child I wondered why he was always down there tinkering around. After all, I wasn't paying the bills—he was! Even though my father didn't carefully articulate the reason he was doing this, he often had me or one of my brothers help him to do this five-minute job of removing and cleaning the filter. His filter was washable and he would replace it maybe once a year.

My father wasn't particularly concerned about "saving energy," but with a house of six children, he was very concerned about "saving money."

A clogged filter means that the heat (or cooling) delivery system is working harder, and inefficiently. Keeping *any and all* appliances working properly can be a big part of efficiently using our resources. This is especially so when heating and cooling a house.

THERMOSTATS

Turn on the heat when you're cold, and turn it off when you're warm. That's what we did in our home growing up, and that's what most folks do. Our mindless lifestyle is what got us into this mess and it is our very mindlessness that keeps us bogged down.

Get a programmable energy-saving thermostat installed in your home, and learn to use it so that you're only heating when you need to. You can program it to turn off when you're asleep, when you don't need as much heat. You can program it to kick on the heater just before you get home on very cold days.

This is an easy upgrade and an easy way to make your home more energy efficient.

FORBES

Glenn Forbes offers the following advice. "For keeping heat inside in the winter," he says, "try to contain the heat to just the rooms you will be sleeping or cooking in by shutting the inside doors. Just by keeping the kitchen door closed, the heat from the refrigerator will warm up that room or the one connected to it."

OFF THE GRID?

Remember, the design of the house, and the insulation of the all the walls, is perhaps the best thing you can do to keep the house cool in summer and warm in winter. There are several places I have lived where I never used any sort of "central heating." This was partly due to the design of the home, and partly because I enjoy a home in winter that is a bit on the cool side, and am content to feel the cold. When it gets a bit too cold, I'll put on a sweatshirt before I will resort to a heat source.

Woodstoves and fireplaces are the obvious heating choices for anyone who doesn't want to use gas or electric heat. And in most parts of the country, you can obtain firewood free, usually year-round, by merely collecting and cutting it yourself.

Though I admit to having purchased firewood on occasion, by planning ahead I have been able to bring home logs from trees that had been cut down, and the wood already cut to woodstove or fire-place size. It's amazing that I was able to find firewood this way, for free. Many times the wood was ready to burn, once it dried. On some occasions, the logs that I obtained for free were large, and I had to take the time to first split the logs with a maul.

You can also produce your own fuel from your yard (or neighbor-hood) by saving all the wood from tree prunings, cut it to size, and stack it to dry.

WOODSTOVES

There are many woodstoves to choose from, and whole books have been written on the possibilities. Before buying a woodstove, you should have an idea of where to place it. The location should heat as much of the house as possible, not just a corner of a room. So the layout of your home may determine what sort of woodstove you will buy.

And though you can go to a fireplace store or catalog and buy any of the marvelous stoves available, I'd strongly suggest you begin by talking to friends who may already have and use a woodstove. Ask them why they selected the model they have, and find out the pros and cons of that model. After a while of doing this, you'll discover that there is no "right" or "wrong" woodstove; there are simply many options depending on your particular situation and needs.

You should also start looking for woodstoves at flea markets and yard sales—you might be surprised how often you'll find these for sale, especially in rural and colder parts of the country where woodstove use is common.

When you see one, start to examine it and ask questions. Is there significant rust? Is there burn-out in certain areas? Do the doors open and close well? Are there pieces missing? Is it only good for heating, or can you cook on the top also? Will it fit in the spot you have in mind? Does it have sufficient height? Will it need to be put on a pedestal? Is it large enough to accommodate the size of firewood you have? Or will you need to cut the firewood into very small pieces? Will you need to buy the smoke pipes, or does the seller have them? Does the look of the stove appeal to you?

In other words, just start examining it very carefully and asking any questions you can think of. The woodstove will become a central part of your home, and you want one that will provide you with years of service without being a nightmare.

Many woodstoves are entirely cast iron, which means they get very hot and retain their heat. Some are made of sheet metal, and these will not last as long. Some are mixes, like some of the early Sears models which were cast iron internally, but then coated in white enamel to look like a modern stove.

Some are covered in layers of soapstone, which is an excellent choice since the soapstone will absorb and radiate heat for hours. You might pay more for such a soapstone stove, but it's well worth it in efficiency.

If you buy a used woodstove, you must examine it carefully inside and out and do your best to get a good deal. Remember, there are only a few reasons why someone would sell a woodstove. One, it might be a smoky stove with broken parts and the owner is tired of it. It might be fine for someone who wants an ornamental object in the yard, but not for you, who wants a workhorse.

Two, it could be an estate sale where someone died and all the furniture is being liquidated.

Three, the stove might be fine but the owner no longer wants the trouble of bringing wood into the house, and then having to deal with all the wood ash on a regular basis. A person with a self-reliant mind-set feels good about doing these things, but there are many reasons why someone will choose to stop doing that (for example, an elderly person who is now living alone).

Four, the city may have become hypnotized by "political correct-ness" and passed a law forbidding woodstoves—yes folks, that *is* a trend. Learn your local laws before you leap into this. Although many people speak "green-friendly," they (meaning, the city authorities) often speak with forked green tongues.

So there are many reasons why you might find a used woodstove for sale. I have purchased new and used woodstoves, and always felt that I got the better deal when I made a careful purchase of a used one.

SAFETY

Of paramount importance is safety. You don't want to burn your house down as the cost of "self-reliance."

So first, you don't put the woodstove directly onto a wood floor. You must lay down a safety layer of bricks, or any special boards used for this purpose. You must not have the woodstove any closer than eighteen inches to the wall, though there are wall protectors designed to allow you to situate the stove a bit closer.

Typically, the smoke piping will go 1. horizontally though the wall, and then up vertically, or 2. straight up vertically through the roof (where there is no ceiling), or 3. (the most common) up through a ceiling and then through the roof. The method you use is determined entirely by where you decide to put your stove.

When I installed our woodstove, I could have used the third method, since we had a ceiling in the living room. However, rather than go straight up vertically, I connected the smoke pipe up nearly to the ceiling, then I put in a 90-degree elbow and ran the pipe about five feet horizontally. Then I put in another elbow for the piping to go vertically through the ceiling and through the roof. This brought more heat into the room, rather than most of the heat simply going out into the night.

There is a special triple-walled insulated device that you want to purchase where the pipe goes through the ceiling, and then another special smokestack where the pipe goes through the roof. Do not try to cut corners here, since you do not want a super-hot pipe touching the wood of your roof and burning your house down.

When you feel everything is safely installed, start a small fire first and test to see if any of the line smokes, which means you don't have a tight seal.

Another safety consideration has to do with children. If there are children in your household, you must find some way to create a barricade around the woodstove so that the child does not get burned.

FIREPLACES

In general, fireplaces are less efficient for heating the home than woodstoves are. This is largely because most fireplaces are designed very simply, and most of the combustible gases end up going right up the chimney. The brick does heat up somewhat and so there is some radiant heat from the bricks after the fire dies down.

The Russian fireplace is a design whereby several baffles are built into the fireplace, slowing the combustible gases so that more heat is radiated into the house. This design is a much more massive fireplace than a typical "ornamental" fireplace, and in some cases, the house is designed around it.

But if you are living in a house where a typical fireplace was built, there are still things you can do to increase the efficiency. I once lived in a house with a fireplace at one end of a very long living room. If you were in the third end of the room that had the fireplace, you'd be warm. But if you were on the other end of the room, you could actually still be cold. We added a grate that was composed of hollow tubes rather than just solid metal. The tubes opened into the room. The idea was that the air in the space inside the tubes was heated, and would naturally flow back into the room. The use of this grate did increase the warming quality of the fireplace by perhaps 15 percent, which was not a great increase, but still noticeable.

I have seen such grates with hollow tubes and some sort of fan that blows the hot air back into the room. This seems like a great idea, though I have never personally tried it.

STEVE LAMB'S ADVICE

Architect Steve Lamb had a little to say about this topic.

"Annoyingly, the state of California has passed regulations against wood-burning fireplaces. The good news there is that if your only heat comes from a wood-burning fireplace, you can use it. For real heat, you need a real masonry fireplace. Those steel zero-clearance things may as well be a television set for all the actual warmth they produce. Real masonry is heated by the wood and stores the heat in the masonry mass and slowly releases it throughout the day. The best of these I have found are the soapstone units. They throw heat out for hours on end. A good hot fire early in the morning and one around dinner time in a real masonry unit located near the physical center of the home will keep you warm in the coldest winter."

AMISH BUILDING PRACTICES

I was first exposed to the Amish when I lived in rural Ohio. Years later, in the late 1990s, I got to go inside many of the Amish homes and workplaces with Peter Gail, who was conducting tours of the Amish countryside.

The Amish eschew nearly all modern appliances, including electricity. They live in this world, but are not of it. All Amish do not hold to identical beliefs about their use of appliances and modern devices, something that Peter once tried to explain to me. Apparently, each local leader can make his own decisions about such matters, and it often revolves around the issue of whether or not the appliance or device will more readily bring in the bad influences of modern society, and whether or not such usage is "prideful." There seems to be a lot of room there for debate and discussion.

All their homes are heated by woodstoves or fireplaces. Part of doing this effectively has to do with how the Amish build their homes in the first place. Most Amish live in Ohio and Pennsylvania, areas that get *very* cold in the winter. The homes are not all crammed together as you see in the city, with no concern at all with alignment to the sun, local wind currents, underground water, and so on. Homes are built to take advantage of the natural sunlight, so large south-facing windows are common, and workshops are also built facing the south.

Houses are built with entryways, vestibules, and service porches, all those pre-entry spaces that also serve as buffers to keep the cold out and the heat in.

Again, the house design is perhaps the single most important factor in creating a home environment that is comfortable in both winter and summer.

It does seem that we are all slow learners who can often barely see beyond tomorrow. We knew about increasing population and dwindling resources fifty years ago, and yes, there were many proclamations and alarming statements, but all the talk did very little to alter our basic way of building homes and building businesses and building cars. It is as if we are schizophrenic, talking the green line with one side of our mouth, but continuing the old status quo when it came to how we choose to make money. This is, fortunately, finally changing, little by little, not by government decree, but by ordinary individuals—pioneers of the quiet revolution—who are choosing to embrace a sustainable lifestyle.

SUMMARY OF SIMPLE WAYS TO KEEP THE HOUSE WARM

Six Very Basic Low-Tech Steps to Keep the House Warm (there are more!)

METHOD	LEVEL OF PRIORITY	RELATIVE EASE TO DO (1 to 5, 1 being easiest)
Insulate ceiling space	Top	Depends on house, 2 to 3
Insulate wall space	High	2 to 4
Insulate floor space	Low	Depends on house, 2 to 3
Fireplace	Medium	Most are inherently inefficient
Woodstoves /wood ovens	High	Quality soapstone woodstoves retain heat through coldest nights
Use double-pane windows	Medium to high	3 to 4, depending on your skill level
Use drapes to cover windows at night	Medium	1

Finally, we should address "homelessness."

Remember, my life experience included a year and a half as a squatter in an unoccupied house whose ownership was being debated in probate courts. Living for next to nothing, I raised food and did countless self-reliance and survival experiments there.

Also, I was homeless for more than six months in a dark time in my life. "Homeless," in my case, did not mean I had no shelter. It meant I had no place to call my own, though I spent the majority of the time sleeping in the basement area of a house, unbeknownst to the owner. I learned to live lean, sleeping in a hammock from the rafter, eating out or from a few select canned goods. And I learned how to wash and stay clean with a hose and cold water. If not sleeping in that basement, I lived in a car. This was neither an ideal nor uplifting experience.

I learned from these experiences, and from all my outdoor camping experiences, that one can certainly "get by" with little or no shelter. Your mind and body learn to deal with no bed, no cover, no toilet, no sink, no safety.

Though I never lived on the street like the thousands of homeless today, I still had a good taste of the misery and danger they experience moment to moment. My experience forever altered the way I perceive the homeless.

In general, there is no meaningful way that the homeless can function and interact in a modern society. Cell phones certainly help in some limited way, as well as solar chargers to keep the cell phone alive. The solution to homelessness, in our non-nomadic society, then, is to do whatever it takes to get off the street, and to seek counseling so that you can alter your thinking and behavior patterns that led to your homelessness. If you drink or take drugs, you must do whatever it takes to stop that suicidal behavior. When you are homeless in a modern society, you are living in a second-by-second crisis emergency, and you are probably not at all able to implement most of the useful suggestions in this book.

Some homeless people are unable to get off the street without assistance. If you are in a position to provide such assistance, it is one of the most worthy jobs to help our fellow men and women to get off the street, and into homes.

Obviously, living a full life and functioning cooperatively in any society necessitates that you have some place that you can call home.

LESSONS I LEARNED FROM A PERIOD OF HOMELESSNESS: FOUR "MAGIC" WAYS TO IMPROVE YOUR FINANCIAL SITUATION

1. Never waste anything!
2. Continually improve your personal honesty/ honorability.
3. Leave every situation or circumstance better than you found it.
4. Tithe to the church (or organization) of your choice.

Yes, I know that some of you will think that these are not solutions at all. That means you have not understood what I have written.

And some of you will declare that you cannot do these things because "I am poor." No! You are "poor" because you do not do these things!

CHAPTER THREE

WATER: THE KEY TO LIFE

SOURCES OF WATER

Historically, villages and cities only sprang up where there was water. You cannot function without a reliable water source. This meant that large population centers would be near a river, a lake, a spring, a well.

But in modern times, we have often tried to fool Mother Nature where we bring the water to the people. If there is not a sufficient amount of local water for the population—as is the case with Los Angeles—then water sources must be found from afar. In Los Angeles' case, this means bringing in water from the Colorado River far to the Southeast, and from the Central Valley of the state, far to the north. Approximately three-quarters of the water needs of Los Angeles are met by three aqueducts, which bring water in from about three hundred miles away!

This means that everyone living in such an area is particularly vulnerable to disruptions of the water supply. These disruptions can occur from an earthquake that breaks the water lines, from terrorist bombings, or simply from a prolonged drought.

Water is essential to life and health. Therefore, having a reliable water source, and/or water storage, should be a mandatory and automatic part of your "survival planning," wherever you live—unless you live in places that are naturally water-rich.

BIG PICTURE

Wherever you live, you should obtain a topographical map from the US Geological Survey. On these maps, water features are found in blue. Examine your map, and look for all the obvious sources of water near where you live. Look for the rivers, streams, and lakes. Look for reservoirs. Try to determine the source of your city's water supply. Look for reservoirs, fountains, water parks.

Also, look at Google Earth and check out your neighborhood. Though I prefer the USGS map for detail, Google Earth will show you all your neighbors who have swimming pools, which would be sources of water in emergencies.

Once you're aware of your local situation, it's time for you to begin storing some water in your home, and determining your local plan for urban self-reliance.

TAP WATER

Since water storage is the most essential, and also the easiest and cheapest step in self-reliant planning, we suggest that you begin by simply storing all the water you can in whatever containers you can get. Really! While some folks can make water storage seem expensive and complicated, you can just fill empty plastic or glass soda bottles (the ones with the screw-on lids), and then store them in a dark place until needed.

Of course, it will be time consuming to fill lots and lots of quart containers, but it is a simple way that you can begin now, without waiting to get big tanks or drums or other specialty containers.

Piped water is hidden in plain view all over the city, and even in remote areas. These keys help you to access that water. They are available at any hardware store.

These juice and water containers were rinsed out when empty, then filled with either tap water, rainwater, or spring water. They are stored in a dark place.

White food-grade bakery buckets can be purchased new, or purchased used and cleaned, and used for water storage. Here is an assortment of recycled containers used to store water.

We have stored water in plastic five-gallon "food grade" bakery buckets. Typically, these are white. These can often be obtained for free or low cost. Clean them, fill with water, seal them securely, and store in a dark place.

We have stored water in thirty- and forty-gallon trash buckets made of heavy plastic. These buckets can be purchased inexpensively when the hardware stores have sales. Make sure the lids fit securely since you don't want to be raising mosquitoes. But to be clear, trash buckets are not regarded as "food grade," and they should be considered as an inexpensive way to get started in storing water for your irrigation and washing needs.

When storing water in plastics, it is a good idea to refill the containers with fresh water at least once a year. There are two reasons for this. One is that most plastics leach into the water. Another concern is that some plastics simply do not last for years and they will get brittle and crack. You need to watch for this or else you may lose all your water.

There are also special water storage containers you can buy at some of the survival specialty stores, as well as at many building supply stores. These are usually blue in color, and described as "food grade." These are great if you can afford them. Buy all you can afford, since you can never have too much water.

Larger food-grade plastic drums allow you to store more water. The large black drums were used to ship pickles into the US. They were washed, fitted with a spigot, and used to store water.

Water is stored in this blue plastic drum. The blue color indicates that the plastic is food grade.

BLEACH

Do you need to add bleach to your water that you intend to store? Bleach is added to retard the growth of algae in the water over long periods of time. Bleach is usually added to stored water so that the green strands or green growths do not appear in their water containers.

Even if you have no bleach, this should not be a serious concern. Green algae is not toxic, and is a cosmetic problem only. You could always strain or boil the stored water if there is excessive algae in the water.

Our experience is that the growth of algae takes quite a while with tap water, probably due to the fact that chlorine is added to the city water before it reaches your sink. If you simply fill containers with tap water, you really don't need to add bleach.

RAINWATER

Perhaps the biggest overlooked water source available to all city dwellers is rain. Though many view the collection of rainwater as "impractical" or "a drop in the bucket," that view is changing. Now the viewpoint is that every little bit helps.

Historically, there have been many communities and nomads who depended, in varying degrees, on rain—or catchments where rain settled—for their water supply. The technology for capturing rain varies from culture to culture, depending on available materials, the local rainfall patterns, the local geology, the presence of other water sources, and so on.

The simplest rain-collecting device that I've seen consisted of a large plastic sheet measuring about four by eight feet, a few clothes pins, and a few five-gallon jugs. After at least thirty-four minutes of heavy rain (to clean the air), you're ready to begin collecting rain. I first witnessed this when woodworker Fred Fryling attached the large sheet of plastic to bushes outside his Venice, California, home. Once the rain began, his jugs quickly filled!

Attach the plastic sheet to bushes so that it is stretched out somewhat, and secure the one point. Place your water jugs under this flow of water, and in a short while, the jugs will be full. A funnel can be helpful. A makeshift funnel can be made from the top of a one-gallon jug. Carefully cut off the top third of the jug and presto!—you have a funnel! A clean piece of cotton can be placed into the funnel to filter out small debris.

The use of clean thirty-gallon trash containers is a bit more practical for the average homeowner. If your house has gutters, simply remove the lower portion of the downspout and place the trash can underneath where it will collect the water.

At one of my past homes that had no gutters, I placed my rain buckets directly under the inside corners of the roof where the water drained off with a heavy flow. Once the rain picked up, the containers quickly filled.

I've also used sturdy five-gallon buckets with handles and lids to collect my rainwater. At a former residence of mine, there was a rather large awning. Due to the construction of the house, much of the roof rain flowed onto the awning, and a heavy flow of rain always flowed from the entire edge of the awning. I would place a line of about seventeen five-gallon buckets at the awning's drip-line and fill all the buckets within thirty minutes to an hour.

In planning your rain collection system, you simply need to observe the flow of rain off of your roof, and position your containers accordingly.

Two things to remember in collecting rain:

1) Always wait at least thirty-four minutes after a heavy rain has begun before you put out your rain catchers. This allows most of the impurities to be washed out of the air, and most of the impurities to be washed off your roof.
2) Always cover the full containers as soon as possible to avoid breeding mosquitoes and other contamination.

FEASIBILITY OF COLLECTING RAINWATER

Still, is this practical and worth all the effort?

The performance of rainwater collection systems over a forty-year period at thirteen California locations was detailed in *Feasibility of Rainwater Collection Systems in California* by David Jenkins and Frank Pearson, published by the California Water Resources Center, University of California, Davis. Quite consistently, it was observed, 88 percent of the annual California rain falls between the November to March wet season. The rain during this wet season is fairly well

These recycled bakery buckets were cleaned, and then placed where rain from the roof's gutters would drain into the buckets. This is a very easy, low-tech method for collecting some of your rainwater.

These buckets were placed close to the house, directly under a rain gutter which drains into the buckets. The rainwater is then filtered before using.

distributed, whereas the scant summer rain is highly variable with no observable pattern of distribution.

The authors of this study pointed out that rainwater collection is certainly possible at most homes. However, when they factored in the cost of storage tanks or barrels, they concluded that storing rainwater might not be cost-competitive compared to piped water.

Relying on the rain as your only or main source of water is possible if you've properly calculated your water needs and have adequate storage tanks. Of course, the weather must also be cooperative for you to achieve a goal of rainwater self-sufficiency.

I've never attempted to rely entirely on rainwater. My concern is simply to save and use some of that freely falling water from heaven. I've rarely collected less than thirty gallons in a single storm, and, on occasion, I've collected as much as four hundred gallons of rainwater in a single downpour. That's water that I can use without relying on the piped water that comes to me from afar. I have always felt that I should use all of the resources that fall upon my little piece of home, and I never wanted the rain that fell on me to be unceremoniously drain out of my yard and down into the city's gutters.

HOW MUCH RAINWATER CAN I ACTUALLY COLLECT?

Let's use an example that's local to me. Even though Los Angeles County is defined as a "coastal desert plain," it receives an average of 14.93 inches of rain each year. Once you know the annual rainfall for your area, you can calculate the potential for rainwater collection in your area.

CALCULATING RAINFALL FOR HARVESTING

1) Measure your roof. And no, you don't need to go up there. In most cases you can just walk the perimeter of the building, and you'll find that the roof's dimensions are the same. So, for example, the roof of my Los Angeles home was about thirty by sixty feet.

2) Thirty times sixty comes out to 1,800 square feet. That is the total possible catchment area. Keep in mind that it's rare that you can actually capture all the rain that falls on your roof.

3) Next, an inch of rainfall on a square foot of surface area yields .623 gallons. Multiply .623 gallons by the number of surface square feet of your roof. In my example, I would multiply .623 x 1800, which equals 1,121. This means that for each inch of rainfall, my roof could potentially collect 1,121 gallons of rainwater!

4) Since the average annual rainfall for Los Angeles is 14.93 inches, I then multiply my roof's potential yield by the inches of rainfall. 1,121 gallons times 14.93 inches annually, and we come up with a potential figure of an incredible 16,736 gallons. That's quite a bit of water that

can be harvested and used for your landscape, drinking water, or other uses. How far would that water last you? Let's say your household of two people uses two hundred gallons of water a day. (Does that sound like a lot? About one hundred gallons a day is the residential average in the US. People tend to use way more water than they think they're using.) So if you divide 16,736 gallons by two hundred, you get about 83 ½ days, which is almost a quarter of your annual water needs.

CAROL KAMPE'S STORY

Recently, I was driving up a local street, which was lined with tall deodar trees and had almost a rural feel to it. I was admiring the beautiful houses and the well-kept gardens and trees, when I noticed it. "It" was totally out of place, though it should be common, something to find at every single home. Rain barrels!

The down-spout of the southwest corner of the house went into a rain barrel. I pulled over to get a better look. This was a large plastic barrel—the type that I'd seen used to import pickles

Kevin Sutherland examines Carol Kampe's rainwater-collection barrels.

Another view of one of Carol Kampe's rain-collection barrels.

into the United States. The entire lid could be screwed off to gain access to the water. The top had been modified with a screen to remove debris that came down from the roof, and a spigot was added to the bottom so one could easily use the collected rainwater.

I had to see the rain barrel up close. I got out of my car and went up to the house, and met the owner Carol Kampe, who was working in her yard. She happily gave me a tour of her rain-collection system.

It turned out that she had not one, but ten rain-collecting barrels strategically located to collect the most rain from the house and garage roofs. Two of the barrels were sixty-five gallons each, and the other eight were sixty gallons each.

The rain thus collected is used for outdoor purposes only—watering her fruit trees and other plants in the yard.

"Generally, I have enough rainwater in my barrels to last me until August," Kampe told me. This means that she is able to rely on the rain for watering her yard for approximately two-thirds of the year. She estimates that she saves perhaps $300 a month in payments to the water company.

"But I don't do this for economic reasons," Kampe adds. "I do it because we live in a desert here in southern California. Water will become more critical as time goes on. So it is just a shame to waste all this good rain."

Kampe has a common-sense approach to her rain harvesting, something that is easy to do and is both ecological and economical. She was living in her home just a few years and then purchased seven of the rain-collecting barrels. She has since added three more. The barrels were purchased for about $100 each from a company that modifies the pickle barrels into rain-collecting barrels. The company also provides hoses so that the barrels can be connected "daisy-chain," so that the overflow of one barrel fills other barrels.

Rain barrels are not light, and water weighs a little over eight pounds a gallon. That means a sixty-gallon barrel full of rainwater weighs in the neighborhood of 480 pounds. So when planning a rain-collecting system like this, one has to recognize that the full barrel is not going to be moved. Other barrels can be connected to the barrel under the downspout so that the overflow can be collected in a spot away from the house.

Also, Kampe is able to simply unscrew the lid of her rain barrels and scoop out water as needed for individual plants. She laughed at all the current talk about "living green," as if it were something new. "We were doing all this back in the 1970s," she says, describing how they recycled and collected rain in Indiana. Emphasizing the need to save and conserve water where you have a desert and an ever-increasing population, Kampe echoes Santyana, pointing out that "anyone who doesn't read history is doomed to repeat it."

RAIN PURITY

In some tests in urban areas, the rainwater contained lead concentrations equal or greater to the limit recommended for drinking water. This was primarily in the northeastern US. Microbiological contamination of rainwater was found to be primarily from bird droppings on the urban roofs.

For these reasons, Jenkins and Pearson recommend that rain collected in urban areas not be consumed, but be used for washing or gardening instead.

I use rainwater for the garden and fruit trees, and for the chickens. I've used it for washing my hair, and it seems to be an excellent hair conditioner. I also regularly consume the rainwater I collect. When I plan to use the rain for drinking, I first meticulously clean those containers well before putting them outside. I'll also cover the opening of the collection container with a sheet of cotton to filter out particles that may wash off the roof. If I forget to add the cotton filter, I'll wait a few hours after the rain stops, and then siphon the rain out of the bucket into a clean jar. I may also run the water through a filter, many of which are sold at backpacking stores.

Due to the general alarm over acid rain, I take the precaution of checking any water that I intend to drink. Test the pH level of the rainwater with a strip of litmus paper which can be purchased at any chemical-supply store, and at some hobby shops. Where I live in Los Angeles County, the rainwater we've collected has almost always been neutral. The one time it tested acidic was because the rain bucket was out and open, and the first rains washing off the roof filled the bucket. That water was full of dirt and whatever was on the roof (dried bird feces, etc.), and it tested acidic. But as long as I follow my standard operating procedure of only collecting rain after at least thirty-four minutes of a downpour, the water always tests neutral.

After a few hours, sediment in the rain-collection bucket settles. Then, the rainwater is poured through a heavy cotton filter into the container, where it is then used for consumption.

Settled rainwater is poured through a heavy cotton filter, filling up plastic and glass quart bottles. This water is then used for soup, coffee, and other food uses.

Michael McKenna pours settled rainwater through a heavy cotton filter, into a larger storage container. The filtered water will then be used for consumption.

DEW

Is dew collection a viable water source in urban areas? It is probably not viable as the only water source, but it could, under certain circumstances, supplement other water supplies.

The simplest form of dew collection would be to mop up the moisture from grass or shrubbery in the early morning. While this is a limited approach, you could collect enough to fill a canteen by simply mopping up moisture in a cotton cloth and wringing it into a container. This method is really more of a last-ditch desperation survival measure.

Morning coffee made with that day's rainwater.

Remember, there is the most dew during periods of fair weather, when you are least likely to get rain.

If you have a metal roof or plastic sheeting on your roof, you will get more dew condensing on your roof. Then, you need rain gutters so that the dew is funneled into an area where you can collect it.

One could also stretch sheets of plastic outdoors between bushes. You need only support the plastic with clothes pins and allow the water to funnel into a container.

COLLECTING WATER FROM THE AIR: DEW COLLECTORS

According to the U.N., nearly 20 percent of people in the world do not have a source for safe drinking water. The result of this is that millions of people die from poor sanitation, and diseases, that are associated with an insufficient water supply. Most of these are children. However, it turns out that in some of the desert regions where there is very little rain, dew and fog are abundant. These are sources of water that are now being "harvested" to produce fresh water for the desert inhabitants.

The collection of fog and dew is not new. It goes back to ancient times. In Israel, for example, archaeologists have discovered low circular walls that were built around plants and vines, which are believed to have been used to collect moisture from condensation. In South America's Atacama Desert and in Egypt, piles of stones have been arranged so condensation can trickle down the inside of the walls where it was then collected.

Dew collects on the unique fabric, and the water drips down a tube and into a collection tank. PHOTO COURTESY OF FOGQUEST.

Since 2001, a Canadian non-profit, FogQuest, has used modern fog collectors to bring drinking water and water for irrigation to rural communities in developing countries. The fog collectors are useful in those regions and deserts which receive less than one millimeter of rain annually. Obviously, in order to be effective, the area must have fog and light winds.

Fog, which is actually a cloud that touches the ground, is composed of tiny droplets of water. How much water is in fog? Each cubic meter contains .05 to .5 grams of water. It doesn't seem like much, but it can add up.

The actual fog collectors have the appearance of a tall volleyball net slung between two poles. The collectors from FogQuest are made of a polypropylene or polyethylene mesh that is especially efficient at capturing water droplets. As the fog rolls through, the tiny droplets of water cling to the mesh, and as the mesh gets more and more saturated, water drips downward into a gutter which channels the water to a water tank.

Fog collectors can also harvest rain and drizzle, and so they are versatile. These particular ones are best suited to high-elevation arid and rural areas. It is not believed that they would work as well in urban areas primarily because the amount of space needed to hang the nets is more the space allows in the average urban lot. Also, per capita water use in the cities of the US tends to be more than the fog collectors could harvest.

Various projects around the world have used from two to one hundred fog collectors. Depending on the details of each site, each net panel can produce 150 to 750 liters of fresh water each day during the foggy season. In the village of Chungungo, Chile, where annual precipitation is less than six centimeters, one hundred fog collectors produced 15,000 liters of water a year for ten years. Also, this water meets the World Health Organization's drinking water standards.

The hills above Lima, Peru, receive about one-and-a-half centimeters of rain each year, with fog from the Pacific Ocean moving in from June to November. FogQuest's project in the village of Bellavista produces 2,271 liters of water a day with seven fog collectors. This supplies sufficient drinking water, and enough water for village residents to have gardens. The hope is that the trees in their gardens will become self-sustaining, collecting their own fog water, reforesting the area and replenishing the groundwater, as trees tend to do "automatically."

The non-profit FogQuest was founded in 2000 by Sherry Bennett and Robert Schemenauer, an atmospheric scientist who has been working on fog collection for over twenty years. The organization is run by volunteers. When a fog collection project is proposed, FogQuest first assesses the conditions of the location to make sure there is enough fog. Since the work of building and maintaining the fog collectors depends on the locals themselves, FogQuest needs a local partner and a community willing to pitch in. If all the conditions are met, the organization builds a small test fog collector, costing from $75 to $200, to see how much water can actually be collected in that location. If the tests show that a sufficient volume of water can be collected there, larger fog collectors of approximately forty square meters can be set up for $1,000 to $1,500 each. These larger collectors can produce up to two hundred liters a day. The system is completely passive, and can last ten years provided it's taken care of.

This technique was also tried in the Atacama desert in northern Chile. It provided all the water the town needed, but required more maintenance than the villagers were willing to put into it, so they eventually switched back to trucked-in water.

Also check the following:

- http://www.sciencedaily.com/releases/2009/06/090605091856.htm
- http://www.aquasciences.com/
- http://science.howstuffworks.com/environmental/earth/geophysics/manufacture-water1.htm

No one thinks that this method would be able to provide the needed water for a city, though there is the chance that water collected by this method could *supplement* city water.

For more details, go to http://www.fogquest.org/. Source for this section was *The Fog Collectors: Harvesting Water From Thin Air*, by Renee Cho, State of the Planet blog by the Earth Institute of Columbia University, March 7, 2011.

WATER FROM AIR CONDITIONERS

Speaking of dew, where does the water come from that constantly drips from an air conditioner during hot weather? Can it be collected and drunk? Is it sanitary?

Did you ever wonder where the water that drips out of AC units comes from? Most of the water dripping from air conditioners is just condensed water vapor that comes from the air inside the building. Air conditioners are designed to drain this water out the back, letting it drip down to the yard or sidewalk. The water from the AC is exactly like rain, which also forms from condensed water vapor. In cases where small amounts of water are left inside a non-operating AC unit, it could stagnate inside the air conditioner and allow bacteria to grow, though this is considered rare.

In a properly functioning air conditioner, the water drips down from the coil into a condensate pan and then exits the unit through a drain or tube. However, if there is a blockage in this drain or tube, water could accumulate inside, which is an ideal environment for many types of harmful bacteria. But again, the water dripping from a properly-running AC unit should be safe to consume.

On a hot and humid day, an average window unit can drip up to two gallons of water, which accumulates on its evaporator coil as it cools and dehumidifies the air. A commercial unit for a business can drip out fifteen to thirty gallons of water a day, depending on its size. This coil, like many drinking water pipes, is made of copper, which explains why air conditioning units are so heavy. Though copper can be unhealthy in high doses, the condensation that drips from air conditioners seems to be low in minerals and dissolved solids.

In 1976, there was an outbreak of Legionnaires' disease that was caused by bacteria that spread out of the air conditioning system at Philadelphia's Bellevue-Stratford Hotel. (The disease got its name from the fact that many of the victims were there attending an American Legion convention.) While *Legionella* is known to thrive in the cooling towers of large air conditioning systems like the one at that Philadelphia hotel, it doesn't seem to grow in smaller units. Furthermore, dripping water isn't really stagnant, so it's extremely unlikely that the water dripping out of it would be infected in any way.

The water that drips from air conditioners is certainly more potable than the drinking water in many countries. The water from an AC unit can also be collected in a bucket and used for irrigation of garden plants.

ANTIGUA COFFEE SHOP OF NORTHEAST LOS ANGELES

DOING LITTLE THINGS TO HELP THE ENVIRONMENT

As I was walking from the old L.A. Farmers Market to get my usual cup of coffee-chocolate at Antigua's, I noticed a new flower bed in the back of the coffee house. Where there was once trash and dead weeds, now there was now a beautiful wood-framed garden bed with colorful flowers and even some vegetables. But there was something different about this approximately six- by six-foot garden space. There was a wooden pole sticking out of the middle, and a plastic bucket was strapped to the pole with some sort of tubing leading to the roof.

I went inside to talk with the owners, Dennis and Miguel Hernandez. The Hernandez brothers were both born in Guatemala City, Guatemala, so they named their coffee house after their home town. (Antigua is the name of the "old" Guatemala City.) They both moved to Los Angeles in 1999 as teens, moving to the US with their father. They both worked at similar jobs, including food industry jobs which got them interested in starting their own coffee house.

After lots of work, they started Antigua at 5703 N. Figueroa in September of 2007.

I saw Dennis and asked him to explain the unique garden out back.

"Oh, you need to talk to Miguel," he told me with a big smile. "It was Miguel's and his daughter's idea."

So the next day, I met with brother Miguel, and we discussed the ecological garden.

Miguel told me that he had wanted to do something with a little bit of space in the rear of the coffee house, a somewhat ugly little spot where trash would accumulate. So, with encouragement and help from his teenage daughter Kathy, he built the little sturdy-framed garden out back.

RECYCLING COFFEE GROUNDS

"You know we throw a lot of coffee grounds away, right?" Miguel asked me. "Well, we filled that little raised bed garden with lots of our coffee grounds. It's a really good way to recycle the grounds." Miguel pointed out that they still end up tossing some used coffee grounds away, because they use so much. They do give some away to gardeners and mushroom growers, and they plan to continually find a home for their used grounds.

SAVING WATER FROM THE AIR CONDITIONING

"But what's that plastic bucket up on the post?" I asked Miguel. He broadly smiled and he told me that he realized the air conditioning for Antigua constantly drips out water. "I ran a tube from the AC to that bucket, and the water from the bucket drips down and waters the garden. Why not put that water to use?" he asked.

Miguel wasn't sure if the AC condensation would be sufficient to water the garden, but to his surprise, he found that the water from Antigua's AC system filled the five-gallon jug at least three times a day, and up to five times during hot weather. "There is so much water coming off the AC," explained Miguel,

Water that flows out of the AC unit at Antigua coffee shop flows into this bucket, where it then flows by gravity into the garden.

The little garden in the rear of the Antigua coffee shop, built from recycled materials, fertilized with old coffee grounds, and watered from water that drains from the AC unit.

"that I run the tube to fill those overflow bottles, and I actually take water home for irrigation."

SETTING AN EXAMPLE

The little garden also has a little solar lamp, and a bird bath for the birds. It's a great example of

Miguel Hernandez and his daughter Kathy work on the little garden in the back of the family coffee shop, watered from the drained AC water.

what anyone—even in the urban environment—can do to help save and recycle resources.

The Hernandez brothers also recycle as many of their used cans as possible, in which they receive certain food items. And during very hot weather, they put out a jug of water and cups on the front entrance for passers-by to get a drink. "A lot of people, even homeless, really need a drink, and sometimes they are a bit too embarrassed to just ask for water," explains Miguel. They also put out a water dish for dogs.

"We're just trying to do the right thing to give back to the community," explains Miguel. "And if we do this, maybe others will do so also, and we'll all make a difference to our community."

WELL WATER

If you have well water, great! Depending on your location, you may need to have it tested from time to time for contaminants, especially in urban areas. If you live higher in elevation than the local urban area, then your water is probably okay, but it should still be tested occasionally. Pollutants tend to flow downstream, not upstream.

Also, if you rely on an electric pump to get your well water, you might consider obtaining a backup manual pump in the event of a power outage.

The *Moher Earth News* online magazine shares how one researcher created a manual pump for his well using PVC pipes. Here is the link to explore: https://www.motherearthnews.com/diy/pvc-manual-well-pump-zmaz00jjzgoe. Or just search around on YouTube if you need to make a manual pump.

LOCAL SOURCES OF WATER

Wherever you live, you should get to know what local sources of water you have in your area. These could be streams, wells, lakes, the ocean, even swimming pools.

If you have a swimming pool in your backyard, you have a pretty good water storage that will last you for some time after any emergency. That water can be used for washing the body and laundry, but FEMA and other health organizations do not advise drinking pool water due to the many toxins that get into the water. However, for a short-term emergency, you could use it sparingly for consumption, but I would definitely boil it before use.

If you'd have to rely on other natural sources of water, you will need to consider how you will actually obtain such water. Will you need to walk to the source? How much water can you actually carry? Remember, water weighs about eight pounds per gallon. What containers will you use? Could you carry some on a bicycle? Do you need to be concerned about looters or muggers?

MORE ON STORAGE OF WATER

Some people simply go to their markets and buy bottled water and put it in the garage. Typically, this is distilled water, though not always. If you choose to go this route, we recommend that you first get a few and, if they are in plastic containers, see how long the plastic actually lasts without leaking. We have seen some plastic containers spring leaks in about six months of storage. Therefore, we strongly encourage you to contact whoever is bottling the water you are considering buying, and ask questions until you get definitive answers. If the best they can tell you is "we don't know," then buy elsewhere.

Or, simply fill your old glass water and juice bottles. Glass more or less lasts forever, and the glass is inert and doesn't react with the water.

WATER HEATERS

The average water heater contains about thirty to fifty gallons of water. If you had no more water coming into your household (for whatever reason), don't forget about that water.

Yes, an on-demand water heater is generally more energy efficient than a water tank. You have to decide what's more important to you: greater energy efficiency, or that extra potential water in the tank. If pipes were broken due to an earthquake, and there was no water pressure coming into your home, you would need to drain the water from the water heater in order to use that water. There is a valve near the bottom of every water heater. It is put there so you can periodically drain the water heater of the rust and sediment on the bottom, and that's how you'd get the water when needed. If the water in one water heater were conserved and used carefully, it could provide emergency water supplies to a family of four for up to a week.

TOILET TANKS

Drink toilet tank water? Hey, as long as you don't use those blue purifying tablets, there is nothing wrong with the water stored in a toilet tank. If nothing else, use it for washing or for your dog. You can still flush the toilet (assuming your drain pipes are not broken) by pouring non-potable water directly into the bowl.

WATER PURIFICATION

Water supplies coming into the urban areas fall into the following categories:

Piped water from local (sometimes not local) water supplies, which the local municipality purifies to some extent before it comes into your home.

Rain, which is seasonal.

Dew (atmospheric moisture), typically a marginal source.

Local open water sources (springs, rivers, streams).

Local stored water (reservoirs).

Other usually marginal sources, such as fountains.

Most water supplies and open sources of water nationwide have shown evidence of some form of contamination, either from human or animal fecal material, or other "naturally occurring" bacteria or viruses. Knowledge of water purification is a must.

WATER PURIFICATION RULE OF FOUR

There are four methods of water purification applicable to your personal use:

Boiling

Sun

Chemicals

Filters

Let's examine each:

METHOD	Process	Pro	Con
BOILING	Put the water into a pot, put on the fire.	Quickly renders suspect water safe to drink.	Must make a fire, which may take time or be difficult. Fire might reveal your position, if that's an issue.
SUN	Put the suspect water into a glass or plastic container, and set in sun.	Low-cost and low-tech way to purify water; can be done with discarded bottles.	Takes about six hours at least.
CHEMICALS	Add the specified amount of chemicals to the water, wait as required.	Relatively quickly renders water safe to drink.	Some people are allergic (or have reaction) to some of the chemicals; sometimes an unpleasant flavor is in water.
FILTERS	Pump (or pour) the water through the filter.	Usually, quite easy to process drinking water through one of these.	They have a finite life, and some are expensive.

BOILING

As every good hobo knows, boiling is the simplest and cheapest way to purify suspect water. Boiling does not in fact kill every living organism in the water. There are a few that actually survive boiling, but just about everything that gets us sick is killed off when you boil the water.

Boiling purifies water, killing harmful organisms in the water.

Boiling is the way you purify water when you are purifying the water from biological contamination. Boiling has no effect on chemical contamination, nor does it render ocean water palatable. To produce drinkable water when there is chemical contamination, or when you are dealing with ocean water, you need a means to distill the water. There are several kitchen distilleries on the market, and numerous low-tech and high-tech methods for distilling water.

SUN

In parts of the world with challenging living standards, clean drinking water cannot be taken for granted.

Though there are many things in the water around the world that can get us sick, the three major health risks to humans found in water are protozoa, viruses, and pathogens. Each one of those categories of water-borne organisms presents their own unique health hazards.

Of these, giardia and cryptosporidium are the most common, and they both pose serious health risks. An infection with these protozoans may cause chronic digestion problems, which lead to malnutrition. Both pathogens have a cystic stage, which makes them resistant to environmental influences, allowing them to survive for long periods of time outside any host.

FIRE IS BEST, BUT NOT ALWAYS POSSIBLE

In the United States, most campers assume water should be boiled for a period of ten minutes, before drinking, just to be safe. In some countries, however, the ability to boil water has proven to be a major obstacle, in large part because of a lack of firewood.

Research shows all pathogens in the water are dead when the water reaches around 170° F (or about 75° C), so, in fact, simply bringing the water to a boil is sufficient.

But what if you simply cannot, or don't deem it wise to, make a fire to purify your water? Is there an alternative?

According to various international agencies, such as EAWAG (Swiss Federal Institute of Environmental Science and Technology) and SANDEC (Department of Water Sanitation in Developing Countries), clear plastic water bottles can serve a valuable role in disinfecting water, generally known as SODIS.

SODIS

This is referred to as SODIS, for SOlar water DISinfection. So how does it work exactly?

The effectiveness of SODIS takes advantage of the sun's UV rays and the process of pasteurization.

Here are the steps.

1. Select a clear PET plastic bottle, free of scratches and dirt. These are relatively common and available worldwide.
2. Fill the bottle three-quarters of the way with clear water and shake to aerate. (If the collected water is cloudy, or contains suspended debris, it should first be allowed to settle in another container, like a bucket. Then, the water should be strained through a cloth before being poured into the plastic bottle.)
3. Fill the bottle the rest of the way and secure the lid tightly.
4. Expose the suspect water to the sun by laying the bottles on their side, either on a roof or somewhere where shadows will not be cast on them, or ideally on a corrugated metal roof.

5. Wait about six hours during full sunlight before you
    drink the water.

LIMITATION OF SODIS

Though very effective, SODIS is not free of limitations. For one, adequate sunlight is necessary.

During winter, when the sun is lower in the horizon, the days are shorter, and the air is cooler, SODIS will take longer to work than during the summer. Cloud cover also means you'll have to keep the bottles out longer than the recommended six hours. Areas in developing countries, between 35 degrees north latitude and 35 degrees south latitude, are ideal for the use of SODIS.

HOW LONG IN THE SUN?

- Six hours if the sky is cloudless or up to 50 percent
  cloudy.
- Two consecutive days if the sky is more than 50 percent
  cloudy.
- One hour at a water temperature of at least 122°F.
- During days of continuous rainfall, SODIS does not
  perform satisfactorily. Rainwater harvesting or boiling is
  recommended during these days.

Cloudy water and water with suspended organic matter—leaves, twigs, etc.—affect the ability of the sun's UV rays to penetrate the water. In those cases, you need to pre-filter the water. If it's really not possible to do this filtering, then you should just heat that water by more conventional means, such as fire.

Also you need to use clean bottles that are dirt-free and free of scratches. Scratches and dirty bottles inhibit the effectiveness of SODIS. Use only clear plastic bottles, not colored bottles.

Standing bottles up does not work well. For maximum effectiveness, you want to lay the bottles on their side and you don't want water deeper than ten centimeters for ideal UV penetration.

It is important to note that SODIS does not produce sterile water. Organisms other than human pathogens, such as algae, are well adapted to the environmental conditions in the SODIS bottle, and may even grow there. However, algae does not pose a danger to human health.

ADVANTAGES OF USING SODIS

Obviously, this is a good method if you do not have the option of building a fire when you want to purify water. You can also process gallons and gallons of water at a time, provided you have enough bottles to do so.

You're not drawing attention to your location by not having a fire, which may be critically important during a period of war or civil unrest. You won't need to expend the energy of searching for firewood. Using SODIS is really easy and anyone can be involved. Use of plastic water bottles for the disinfection of water seems like a very effective, low-tech, low-cost method people can use wherever and whenever the need may arise.

There is quite a bit of science behind SODIS, far beyond the scope of this article. For those interested, more information can be found

A demonstration of the SODIS method in Indonesia.

Plastic liter bottles set out in the sun to practice the SODIS method.

Tracy examines a bottle of water laid out in the sun, as per the SODIS method of water pasteurization.

at http://www.sodis.ch/meth-ode/anwendung/ausbildungs-material/dokumente_material/manual_e.pdf.

CHEMICALS

WATER PURIFICATION PILLS

There are several water purification pills sold at pharmacies and backpacking stores. Though these are reliable when very fresh (under two years old), they lose their efficacy when exposed to heat, and as they age.

IODINE CRYSTALS

Iodine crystals are soaked in a certain amount of water, and that solution is then used to purify contaminated water. Iodine crystals, properly stored, have an unlimited shelf life. As long as you still have some crystals in your water, the solution you produce will still be able to kill biological contaminants in the water.

Chemical methods of water purification do exactly what boiling does, except with chemicals. That is, in both cases you are drinking dead bacteria (assuming there were contaminants in the water in the first place).

However, iodine crystals themselves are toxic and are getting harder to obtain, mostly because they are used in illegal drug laboratories. Pregnant women and people who have had thyroid surgery are not advised to use this method of water purification.

COMPARING FOUR WATER TREATMENT METHODS

Source: www.cdc.gov/healthywater

Contaminant	Boiling	Filtration	Iodine/Chlorine	Chlorine dioxide
Cryptosporidium (Protozoa)	Effective	Effective	NOT effective	Effective
Giardia (Protozoa)	Effective	Effective	Effective	Effective
Bacteria (e-coli, salmonella, et al.)	Effective	Effective	Effective	Effective
Viruses (hepatitis, enterovirus)	Effective	NOT effective	Effective	Effective

FILTERS

WATER PURIFICATION STRAWS

These are interesting devices that are inexpensive and possibly useful in limited situations. They are handy, easy to carry, and usually work via a charcoal filter. However, they should be used once, or over the course of a weekend, and then discarded. If stored for awhile after use, they can breed bacteria, and actually be the source of contamination.

SINK-TOP WATER PURIFIERS

There are many commercially available water purifiers available. We feel confident that most do what they claim to do. Be sure to read the containers and ask questions so you are buying what is right for your needs. For example, is there a replacement unit that you will need to buy? What is the cost of the replacement filter, and how often do you need to replace it? What does your filter remove, and what does it not remove?

Brita and PUR are two popular brands for use in the kitchen.

BACKPACKING FILTERS

We are reasonably confident that all of the water filters sold at backpacking stores will do what the manufacturers claim. The price range is from about $25 to about $250.

We suggest you look at what is available, ask for a demonstration if possible, and determine what your particular needs will be before making a purchase. Katadyn filters are widely regarded as the Cadillac of water filters, with the most expensive price tags. They are the best. However, the manufacturers of First Need claim that their filters not only do everything that the Katadyn does, but that First Need does some things even better. First Need filters start at about $60. And then there is the inexpensive Timberline filter, which is easy to use, and handles most, but not all, water-contamination situations.

By the way, over the years, we have collected a thick file of "lab test data" from the various manufacturers of backpacking filters. It is difficult to compare, since each company seems to hire its own lab to show that their product is the best. To date, we have never seen an independent lab analysis of all the popular filters on the market. To be meaningful, they would have to start with a sample of water with known, measurable contaminants, and then test the water again after it has been through the filters.

We can say that it does appear that you get what you pay for, though you don't always need the most expensive.

WATER CONSERVATION

If water is scarce for some reason, there are quite a few things you can do to stretch that water. Even if the water is not scarce, if you're trying to practice the ecological principles of permaculture, you're going to want to let all the water you use indoors also feed your plants outdoors.

Let's hear what Dr. George Fischbeck has to say about the subject of water conservation. For many decades, Dr. Fischbeck was a popular television weatherman. He wrote the following when California was experiencing a drought. It's reprinted here with permission.

SOLUTIONS from DR. GEORGE FISCHBECK

Folks, do you know that this densely populated Southern California urban sprawl is located on what geologists call a "coastal desert plain"? That's right—we live in a desert. And yet we use and waste water as if there is no tomorrow. If we don't start realizing where we live, we're bound to have some severe problems in the near future. Why? Because everyone wants to live in Southern California. And where does the water come from? From Northern California and from the Colorado River. Water experts tell us that we might have a real crisis on our hands real soon if we don't learn to live with less water.

I want to assure you that I'm not a "doom and gloomer." I'm ever-hopeful that we can rise to the occasion and become part of the solution. The solution, although made to seem overly complex by some "experts," is within reach of you and me. Our solution is to follow the old dictate: Waste not, want not. And making the solution a part of our daily lives needn't be a sad burden. Implementing practical solutions can and should be a joy-filled exciting activity.

Let's explore some of the ways in which everyone can pitch in and help.

Did you know that nearly 50 percent of our residential water use is literally flushed down the toilet? Today there are toilet tanks that can flush with less water, and some areas are now requiring these in new construction. And if you don't feel ready for going out and buying a water-saving toilet, you can get a free kit from the Department of Water and Power; it includes a plastic bag of water which you put in your toilet tank so that you use less water with each flush.

An innovative group in Highland Park named White Tower Inc. (WTI) has been practicing a unique form of water conservation for nearly seventeen years. The household members save their bath and shower water in one-gallon containers, which they neatly store in the bathroom. Then, using specially-cut plastic pour containers, they use their bath and shower water to flush the toilet. This is a simple method of water conservation that even apartment dwellers can practice.

Of course, whenever your faucet or sink runs needlessly, you've got to just turn it off. Need new washers? Washers are easy to replace, and you really shouldn't need to call a plumber for such a simple task. However, if you're uncertain how to do it, call that plumber but watch him and have him show and tell you how to fix that washer the next time.

Did you know that some plants in your yard require much more water than others? Talk to the people at your local nursery, and find out which plants are drought tolerant. Many of the native plants are drought tolerant and are quite attractive. A drought-resistant landscape needn't be drab and plain—there are many, many desert-dwelling plants that are fragrant, attractive, colorful, and in some cases, even edible, as with the prickly pear cactus fruits.

If you have a yard, you should seriously consider grey-water recycling. Grey water refers to the water that goes down our kitchen and bathroom sinks, and down the tub. With some simple drain-line alterations, and with the possible change of detergent, you can direct this once-used water into your yard to water your trees, bushes, and even garden.

But keep in mind that grey-water recycling is restricted in some areas, so you'll need to check with local plumbers and city hall for more details. Although grey-water recycling is an excellent way to "use water twice," it's gotten a bad reputation because some people allow it to become a health hazard.

Improper grey-water recycling can result in your breeding mosquitoes, for example. (As an aside, did you know that the original navel orange tree in Southern California was planted outside a home and watered with dishwater? You can still see that tree today in Riverside!)

Also, remember that ideally you should do your yard watering at night when there is less evaporation.

The number of ways in which we can save and conserve water are endless. Some ways that most of us don't usually think of are, for example, collecting rainwater from your roofs in plastic trash buckets—just like "grandma back on the farm" used to do, right? Your editor told me that he has collected up to four hundred gallons of rainwater in a single storm, although usually he collects about forty gallons of rain a storm. That's free water that doesn't have to be imported to us.

Another novel idea has actually been around since the '20s. The Kozak Company in New York manufactures a product called the Auto DryWash cloth, readily available at hardware and auto supply stores. It actually "washes" your car without water. The big city fleets and car lot owners really ought to be using a product like this!

Folks, remember that we can always lick a problem if we stick together and work together. At your Neighborhood Watch meetings, you should discuss with your neighbors all the ways you can save and conserve water. Don't wait for "the government," since the solution is really within our own grasp.

I am hopeful for our future. And thank you for letting me share my ideas with you!

Dr. George Fischbeck
Meteorologist, KABC TV

[*Reprinted with permission from Dr. George Fischbeck, former TV meteorologist in the Los Angeles area.*]

WATER RECYCLING RETROFITTING

During my early association with Mr. White's non-profit WTI, we focused upon principles of what are now called "sustainability." In other words, we wanted to utilize as many of the resources that came onto our property wisely. We wanted all the rain that fell there to stay there. Water was piped in from afar, and we wanted even that waste water to go to work, double-duty, growing the trees and garden.

I worked with Timothy Hall in order to disconnect the bathtub drain pipe from the sewer line in the house and attach pipes so the bath water would drain about one hundred feet away into the orchard area. It didn't take much time to disconnect the drain from under the bathtub, but we did have to crawl under the house in the narrow crawl space, getting covered with cobwebs and this very fine decomposed granite that stained our clothes and didn't wash out. Then, we used old recycled galvanized pipes and connected the pieces until we had a line going all the way downhill to where trees would be planted for an orchard. This took us the better part of the day. Forever after, all the water from the tub went directly into the lower orchard, and only "safe" detergents were used—those that had no dyes or aromas added.

At this time, Timothy operated a local health-food café, and on the bulletin board we advertised ourselves as "ecology plumbers" who would go to your home and retrofit your sink or bathtub drain so the water would go outside. We knew this was illegal according to the Building and Safety codes of the City of Los Angeles at the time, but there was also a drought during this time, and people wanted to get as much use out of their water as possible. Timothy and I did a half-dozen or so of these jobs to the delight of renters and homeowners.

The City of Los Angeles representatives made a lot of noise about the people saving water and using less. The news notices of the day talked about a lot of very standard ways to save water: turn off the water when brushing teeth, water your yard at night, plant drought-tolerant plants, use lots of mulch, don't wash off the sidewalk, use a full load when you wash clothes, etc. But through my work with Timothy and WTI, we went way beyond those very basic ways to save water. And we taught others how to do likewise.

We strongly advocated against having a front lawn, one of the biggest and pointless water wastes in the entire country. We collected rainwater in our own low-tech way. We washed a few items of clothes every time we took a bath. And we altered our own plumbing so that the kitchen and bathtub water could flow right outside into the garden. And it turned out that this last method—known today as "grey water recycling"—was then, and might still be, illegal according to the Department of Building and Safety of the City of Los Angeles. The rationale for this being illegal is that everyone has their own way of doing it and some folks are less careful than others. The city didn't want pools of water outside homes and apartments which raise mosquitoes and possibly attract rats or roaches or worse.

Still, we focused on kitchen sink and bathtub water, and we only did it where it could be done easily by gravity and where it would not be a problem. In one case, we disconnected the drain from under a second-story kitchen sink, and attached a PVC drain pipe that had to go through the wall to the outside. We had to drill an appropriate-sized hole, and then we attached the hardware to it that would allow the owner to screw on a garden hose. The garden hose was then moved around as needed by the homeowner so that the water would flow under fruit trees, ornamentals, or the garden.

We advised the customers that they should only buy dish soaps that contained no dyes or perfumes. Phosphates weren't a big issue, as they are when your detergents flow into the Los Angeles County sewer system, and eventually flow out to the ocean. Phosphates in the soil act as a fertilizer. Timothy and I were delighted to do some part-time work that we enjoyed, and we felt made a difference in the world. Furthermore, for a few hours' work, I would earn close to $50, which made me think I was pretty close to a millionaire for the day.

I did this same retrofit at the cinder block house on top of the hill which was my home. This was very easy to do, as there was a clean-out valve just outside the kitchen, and all I needed to do to capture most of the drain water was to attach a line to that clean-out pipe, and run the line out into the yard. Though this didn't recycle all the water from the kitchen sink, it did send perhaps 60 percent of the water going down the drain into my yard and garden. Eventually, I moved the drain line out into the larger yard to the south.

Since I had potted plants and a little nursery just outside the kitchen door, I would simply take the plastic dish pan when done washing dishes, and empty the water onto the plants. This is probably one of the easiest ways to recycle household water with no cost of retrofitting. It is really a no-brainer—even my mother did that consistently at her Pasadena home, and would yell at me and my brothers if we did not do so. "Why are you so lazy?" she'd chide us. "Take that water outside and water the roses!"

Those early retrofits with Timothy had a lasting impact on me, because in the beginning the whole idea of grey-water recycling was a big mystery to me. After doing so many of the retrofits—and each one was unique—I realized that grey-water recycling is one of the easiest things to do. After I left the cinder block house on top of the hill, I eventually owned my own home, and found that it was easy to recycle the washing machine water and kitchen water.

Later, in another home, I did the same thing with the washing machine, and kitchen, but not the bathtub because there was no way to use gravity for the water to flow outside. Later still, at a house I rented, I sent all the kitchen and bathwater out into the yard. I mulched heavily and would often toss seeds right out the kitchen window. When I finally left this little cabin in Altadena, a fifteen-foot avocado tree had grown in about five years from one of my seeds that I'd tossed out the window, and was producing fruit with no grafting.

It made sense then, and it makes sense now, to recycle all one's water. And despite all the smiley talk and encouragement from the folks at city hall, the right hand of the city does not always agree with the left hand. If and when Building and Safety finds out you are doing "illegal" grey-water recycling, you'll be cited and asked to hook back up to the sewer. The alternative is to buy the pumps and holding tanks they now require for this, and the expensive permit, upwards of about $10,000. And that price means that anyone smart will simply not talk to city hall, but find ways to "go green" safely and inexpensively.

Perhaps today because there are more and more of us residing on smaller and smaller parcels of land, many of the simple and common-sense things that we just did with no regard for any government dictates or rules are not as possible today. This isn't because it's not a good idea, but rather because not everyone takes the time to recycle and to compost in a way that is hygienic and sightly.

GREYWATER RECYCLING SUMMARY FROM FIVE HOUSEHOLD SOURCES

Every situation is different, and this assumes you have the yard space to recycle the water into.

	COMMENTS	DIFFICULTY*	PRO	CON
KITCHEN SINK	Requires using non-toxic detergents.	2–3	Food scraps act as fertilizer for garden.	Grease might attract vermin.
BATHROOM SINK	Toothpaste, mouthwash, and other substances used here.	2–3	Typically, easy to do, and can provide regular water for trees.	Because of the substances that go down this drain, make certain it exits in a safe area.
BATHTUB/ SHOWER	Typically one of the easiest retrofits; must use safe soaps.	2	Easy to do; provides regular water for yard irrigation.	Be mindful of shampoos, conditioners, et al., that go down the drain.
WASHING MACHINE	Must have the yard space for a large volume of water.	3	Easy to do and provides large volume of water for irrigation.	Be mindful when you purchase laundry detergents.

	COMMENTS	DIFFICULTY*	PRO	CON
DISHWASHER	We advise against having dishwashers.	2–3		Water may exit very hot.
TOILET	N/A			

*: 1–5, 5 being most difficult

Whatever the argument, I still believe that the simplest path is the best, and that the most natural course of action is the most ideal for the most people. That which has worked for millennia should still work as long as people are willing to slow down, and quit their blind faith in a technological god that they think will miraculously save us.

WHAT DID I LEARN?

1. List three sources of water if suddenly you turn on the tap and nothing comes out.
2. List three ways to purify water in your backyard.
3. Is the water that drips from your air conditioner safe to drink?
4. Is pool water safe to drink?

CHAPTER FOUR

FOOD: GROWING YOUR OWN, AND STORAGE PRINCIPLES

SOURCES OF FOOD

How can you utilize whatever yard space you have to produce at least some of your food? Once you start to do this, you might be surprised that food plants can be grown just about everywhere. You'll rip out your front lawn and plant a garden and mini-orchard, and never look back.

FRUIT TREES

Whenever you do landscaping, always think about your ability to be self-reliant. Insist on planting trees that produce food, or produce medicine, or produce wonderful fragrance, or are useful in some other way. Many times you can find trees that fulfill two or more of these needs. Don't let a landscaper or gardener plant a tree that is "popular" or simply because he says it "fits the motif of your yard." Insist on planting useful plants. Even roses are useful since the flowers and fruits are rich sources of vitamin C.

If you have limited experience in creating a yard that produces your own food and medicine, I suggest you begin by first meeting with a good nurseryperson and getting a list of those trees that do well in *your* specific area.

You should get two lists: One list should be all the native trees of your area, and the second list should be all the standard fruit and nut trees that will do well in your area. Examine the lists carefully. Natives trees, by definition, will do well where you live. You should try to select as many trees from that list as possible. Choose the ones that appeal to you, whose fruits you are likely to eat and enjoy.

The apple is a good choice just about everywhere.

"HIP"s

Some folks insist on growing ornamentals. If your intent is to create a self-contained, closed-system permaculture style system on your property, you would never grow a plant simply because it is an "ornamental," whose appearance you find attractive. Everything should have a use.

Still, the city is already full of many trees and shrubs that produce food, but which were planted primarily as "ornamentals." My wife Helen came up with the term "HIP" for these—"horticulturally introduced plants." I document many of these in my book, "Nuts and Berries of California" (Falcon Guides, 2015), and the vast majority of the HIPs we discuss are found nationwide.

Here are some:

Roses (Rosa spp.) are found nationwide. We have wild roses, and many varieties of cultivated roses. The fruits and flowers are edible.

Roses are found in the wild and are common in urban gardens. The "hips" (fruits) and the flowers are both edible.

Figs (Ficus spp.) go feral quite easily and these trees to small bushes are found in diverse places. The ripe fruits are edible.

Loquats (Eriobotrya japonica) is widely planted as an ornamental, and its yellow fruit is delicious and commonly made into jams. Most people who have these will allow you to have all you want, if you ask first.

Mulberries (Morus spp.) are another common tree nationwide, with its characteristic fruit, either white or black.

Loquat trees are easy to grow, and they produce early sweet fruit.

ACORNS AND OTHER NATIVES

And there are many others. Learn about the uses of the plants where you live, and then begin to try them one by one.

Besides learning about the HIPs, you should take the time to learn the many wild and native plants that grow near you. I am particularly fond of using acorns for food, which drop from oak trees worldwide every autumn.

Following traditional methods, I shell the acorns, and then grind them into a flour. I put that flour into a sieve into which I have placed a tea cloth. (Think of this as a manual coffee-maker, where you pour the water into the grounds). I pour cold water into the acorn flour which leaches out the bitter tannic acid with the water. I taste the acorn flour, and when it is no longer bitter, I can then make bread or pancakes, or dry and store the flour for later.

A bowl of acorns, ready to be processed into edible flour.

Angelo Cervera grinds the shelled acorns on a traditional metate. The raw flour will still need to be leached of bitter tannic acid before being used in bread or pancakes.

GARDEN

Yes, plant a garden! There are garden clubs all across the country to help you with what is best in your part of the country. And there must be thousands of books on gardening to help you with all aspects of producing food in your own backyard.

Here is what I do. I grow the plants that are easy to grow, and grow well in my area. Period. Well, not exactly "period." I do begin with a list of all the plants that I'd ideally like to have in my idealized yard to provide me with all my food and medicine and fragrance. Then I delete those which I know will not stand a chance because they are too adapted to a different environment, or because they need too much care, which they will not get with me. I begin with the natives that are on my list because I already know they will grow here. I am not trying to tempt fate.

Then I select the fruits and vegetables which are the most likely to survive in my environment, with minimal care. The "minimal care" thing is my personal choice, and if you enjoy spending long hours tying up vines and making sure there's not too much mulch under trees, and making sure there's just the right amount of moisture and sun, that's fine—for you. I do not have the luxury of spending long hours in the yard.

THE PERENNIAL GARDEN

After studying my criteria, I know I can include all onions and garlic, and nearly all herbs. New Zealand spinach is a ground-cover spinach relative that grows very well here. It's also a perennial and never needs to be replanted once planted. I like that. There is a New Zealand spinach patch that I planted which has consistently produced now for over thirty years.

Jerusalem artichokes continue to multiply "like weeds" once established, and each plant will produce buckets of tubers each year. They are native to the eastern US and North America, and do well as long as the soil is not too dry and hard. Squash plants, tomato plants, pepper plants, all seem to do well for us with minimal care.

Every front and back yard can have a garden. Even in a small space, you can grow a little bit of your own food.

New Zealand spinach is a perennial which produces greens year-round.

Learn to grow those plants that you enjoy, but also those plants that tend to grow well in your yard, with minimal care.

WEEDS

Someone seeking a self-reliance lifestyle wouldn't bother with a front yard, but would use that space for a food garden. And in North America, many (if not most) of the "weeds" that appear in your garden are edible and good. Many are seasonal; some are annuals and some perennials.

Here is just a sampling of some of the common weeds typically found in gardens which can be eaten:

Chickweed (Stellaria media), a great salad plant.

Chickweed is found throughout North America in the spring and makes a great salad plant.

Lamb's quarter (Chenopodium spp.), a spinach relative whose leaves can be eaten raw or cooked. Seeds are edible too.

Nettles (Urtica spp.) is a European native found widespread in the spring. The nutritious leaves are good in soups, cooked dishes, and tea.

Sow Thistle (Sonchus spp.) is a tall relative of dandelion whose leaves are good in salad or soup. It's widespread in gardens and empty spots.

Lamb's quarter is another widespread garden weed, which can be used raw or cooked, just like you'd use spinach.

Stinging nettle is widespread in wild areas and in gardens. It's a delicious cooked green.

This student is holding a stinging nettle because it doesn't bother him—but you should wear gloves when you collect nettles.

Wild onions (Allium spp.). Many species are found in North America. They look like grass and you can smell the obvious onion smell when crushed.

There are many, many others. I strongly suggest you get a field guide to wild edible plants of your area, and start taking field trips with an ethnobotanist so you can learn how to properly identify the plants.

I have written many books on the uses of wild plants, such as "Guide to Wild Foods and Useful Plants," "Foraging Wild Edible Plants of North America," and others. Please get a copy!

SOIL

If you have never gardened, just remember that the key to healthy, insect-resistant plants is good soil. You MUST make a compost pit of some sort, and enrich your soil. And you should focus upon the basic principles of permaculture, and find ways to create your compost from the plant wastes from your own yard (leaves, kitchen scraps, etc.). You must be constantly finding ways to enrich the soil, to make it more arable, to make it friendly to earthworms, and to make it friendly to your garden plants.

Many years ago, I participated in a call-in radio show about gardening, and I also participated in the seminars held by the radio host. I was often asked questions for which I was expected to have an answer. By far the most common question was, "What can I do so that my African violets grow better?" or, "What can I do so that my azaelas have better flowers?" In other words, *most* people wanted to know how to make a specific plant grow better and be less prone to disease and insect infestation. In all cases, the gardeners were asking the wrong questions. I almost never directly answered the question about the African violets and the endless list of plants, but rather I began to ask them what they did to their soil, and how they improved the soil. I also inquired about whether they had eucalyptus trees growing nearby (most plants do very poorly under eucalyptus trees), available sun, wind patterns, and quality of the soil. My advice was very predictable: Improve the soil and everything growing there will improve. Also, top quality soil renders the plants growing there more drought tolerant, more frost tolerant, and more insect resistant.

Still, in some cases, the gardeners were not content with my answers and wanted more. I would tell them that perhaps the African violets they were trying to grow were inappropriate to their ecosystem, and that they should reconsider growing something more useful and appropriate to their area. Those who were intent upon replicating the appearance of a garden they saw in some popular gardening magazine had little use for my advice, and never called back.

Today, there are libraries of books on gardening techniques, as well as many online sources of information. I suggest you contact a local organic gardener, neighborhood garden, or local gardening club. That way, you can see first-hand how to garden, and what plants do well in your local area.

GROWING OYSTER MUSHROOMS

This is the story of how one man grows his own edible mushrooms in his home using old cardboard and used coffee grounds.

Matt Heidrich is a man who loves oyster mushrooms. He enjoys them so much that he has learned the intricate art of home cultivation. I didn't know what to expect when I visited him at his home in the hilly section of northeast Los Angeles, but I certainly got a full tutorial.

Oyster mushrooms are a variety of mushroom that grows on old and dying trees throughout

Matt Heidrich with some of his home-grown oyster mushrooms.

the nation. They grow from the sides of trees with gills that slope down to meet the stem. The caps range from cream to dark brown. They are one of the simplest mushrooms to cultivate, and enjoyed by mushroom enthusiasts and foodies alike. I always assumed they were called oyster mushrooms because the flavor (to me) is very much like oysters, though some say the name derived from the shape of the mushroom's cap being similar to an oyster shell.

A child of army parents, Heidrich spent his childhood in Indiana, and it was there that he first found and harvested some of another wild mushroom in the woods—the popular and colorful chicken-of-the-woods.

In 2015, at Los Angeles' eclectic EcoVillage, he attended a workshop where he was introduced to the lifestyle of fungi. The workshop included the details for cultivating the oyster mushroom, and Heidrich was hooked. Over the last several years, he has refined and perfected his technique for producing oyster mushrooms in his home.

When I first visited Heidrich, I was given a tour of his small backyard, where he grows numerous herbs and vegetables in small upraised beds. In one corner was a small compost pile covered with black plastic, which he uses mostly for the old medium of which his mushrooms grow. He pulled up a corner to show me that oyster mushrooms abundantly grew from his little compost pile, the unexpected result from the leftovers of his cultivation. He picked a few of the good ones for his meal later in the day.

Next, we went indoors for the tutorial. It was quickly evident that growing oyster mushrooms was important to Heidrich, because it appeared that major portions of at least two rooms in his home were devoted to the various stages of oyster mushroom cultivation.

We began by looking at some of the good textbooks that are available on the subject. Two of the best current books on mushroom cultivation are *Growing Gourmet and Medicinal Mushrooms*, by Paul Stamets, and *The Mushroom Cultivator*, by Stamets and Chilton. *Radical Mycology*, by Peter McCoy and *Organic Mushroom Farming and Mycoremediation*, by Trad Cotter are also very useful. And for those who want to buy starter kits, Stamets' company, called FungiPerfecti, provides supplies for beginner and expert alike.

There are many ways to cultivate mushrooms. The novice grower does not use spores, but spawn, which is genetically identical to the parent mushroom. Most home growers use liquid culture spawn and grain spawn. Liquid culture is simply mushrooms grown in sugar water. Grain spawn is mushrooms grown on grain. Heidrich cultivates his liquid culture using simple sugars purchased from the local homebrew shop. (In fact, homebrewing and mushroom growing go hand in hand.) For grain spawn, he uses organic wheat berries bought in bulk on Amazon. The goal of these methods is to give the mycelium (the mushroom body) the nutrients it needs to form robust fruiting bodies ("fruiting bodies" are what most of us simply call mushrooms). Liquid culture and grain spawn are readily available on eBay or from mushroom websites. The simplest way to begin cultivating is to buy liquid culture online and expand it at home in modified Mason jars. But cleanliness is key.

Heidrich created his own sterile environment with a five-gallon clear Rubbermaid tub, onto which he has added two holes where his hands can enter with gloves. Into this box, after he has disinfected it with alcohol, he adds the starter medium, and several Mason jars of wheat berries which will be inoculated with the liquid starter medium.

He carefully closes the lid of the box, and once everything needed is inside the box, he dons his gloves and his hands enter the box. The lid of each jar has had two holes drilled into it: one hole is stuffed with cotton for aeration, and the other is filled with high-temperature RTV engine silicone. With a hypodermic needle, he first sucks a measured amount of the liquid out of the starter

The Mason jar for the starter medium.

medium, by pushing the needle through the silicone cover, and then he injects a measured amount into each jar of the wheat berries, again, by pushing the needle through the silicon layer.

This is all done very carefully, almost like a careful dance as Heidrich maneuvers into the limited space. But all this is necessary; otherwise the invisible contaminants in the air and environment will infect the batch of mushrooms.

When done, Heidrich places these inoculated bottles of wheat berries onto a rack with an LED light to assist in stimulating the grown of the spawn. Temperature requirements vary depending on the oyster variety. For example, there are blue oysters which prefer a cooler temperature, while the pink and phoenix oysters enjoy temperatures up into the 80s and 90s.

After a few weeks, if all has gone well, the bottles of wheat berries are covered in a white cob-webby material, which is the mycelium that will produce the mushrooms.

The needle with the starter medium, left, to be injected into the medium in the jar.

Getting everything ready to inoculate the wheat medium.

Heidrich takes such a bottle to show me how he sets up the final stage of cultivation, which can take place in a plastic bag or bucket. Today he demonstrates in a plastic bag.

Into the approximately gallon-sized plastic bag, he places a layer of soaked cardboard. (I had noted earlier that he had a few containers of old cardboard in his backyard, and this is what he uses to grow his mushrooms.)

"Remember, these mushrooms like to grow on wood, and isn't that what the cardboard came from?"

Working inside the sterile box.

smiles Heidrich. He presses a layer of cardboard into the bag, and then adds a layer of used coffee grounds, a free recyclable material from a local coffee house. Then he adds about five tablespoons of the wheat berries covered in spawn. Then he adds more cardboard, more coffee grounds, and more spawn. He continues this way for several layers until the bag is full. On his last, upper-most layer, he adds only spawn, then cardboard, then spawn. Heidrich explains that the coffee grounds are most susceptible to infection, and by having no coffee grounds at the top where it is exposed, there is less chance of infection.

Once this is sealed, Heidrich punches a few holes into the bag so that each hole enters the bag at the cardboard. Once the mushrooms get growing, they will grow out of the holes where they can be easily harvested. This bag is again put on the shelf with the LED light, and allowed to sit until the mushrooms start to grow.

It all seems like a very mysterious process, but Heidrich is merely controlling in a scientific manner that which occurs naturally in the forest.

Cardboard soaking in water in a plastic bucket.

Heidrich's favorite method of preparation is to sautee the mushrooms with his meals.

"How do you preserve the surplus?" I asked him, innocently enough.

"I eat them as quickly as I grow them," he said smiling. "There's never a surplus!"

Wow! He loves his mushrooms. Nevertheless, if growers have a surplus, they can be frozen or dehydrated, and dehydration seems to be the preferable choice.

He's not a vegan, vegetarian, macrobiotic enthusiast, or a food faddist of any sort. "Yes, I eat meat," with a smile that barely

A plastic bag is filled with layers of cardboard, old coffee grounds, and the medium. Once the bag is full, Heidrich punches a few holes in the bag and then lets it sit on a shelf until the mycelium grows.

A bag where the mycelium is now growing through the cardboard, and the oyster mushrooms will soon pop out of the holes in the bag.

conceals a bit a guilt. He's a man who loves one of nature's finest foods, and he's found a way to have a constant supply at home.

Heidrich offers occasional workshops where he takes participants through the various steps involved. His workshop participants walk home with an instruction sheet, and a bag of spawn to grow at home. For more information, he can be reached at mattheidrich@gmail.com.

BUYING FOOD

Let's get real basic here. There are folks who can pop down several hundred to several thousand dollars for boxes of food from the companies that sell "food storage systems." These are the companies that you see advertising in such magazines as *Mother Earth News, Countryside, Organic Gardening*, and many of the other survival-oriented publications. If you are in a position to make such a purchase, do so! For the most part, buying in bulk makes good economic sense, and you don't need to run to the store every day.

But, many more people simply cannot afford to spend large sums of money all at one time. Then what?

SUPERMARKET BUYING

We strongly suggest that you watch for specials and sales at your local supermarket, and buy two, three, four times what you would ordinarily buy. We have used coupons as well, and have routinely saved 30 to 50 percent from the retail prices of the food items. We never clip coupons for products we don't actually use, however, since that becomes a false economy.

The general rule of thumb for food storage is the BUY WHAT YOU EAT and EAT WHAT YOU STORE (meaning, rotate).

Don't buy frozen goods when considering long-term storage. Everything must be dried or canned. Most modern canned goods will last up to ten years, with the exception of tomato products, which often leak after three or so years.

Remember, you aren't necessarily storing food in case of an emergency—though that idea is always there in the back of the mind. But it's also more economical to buy in bulk, so the unit cost is less, and so you are not wasting time (and fuel) on so many extra trips to the store.

BUY DIRECT FROM FARMERS

In most parts of the country, there are more and more farmers' markets where you can buy direct from the farmers. Though they typically offer their produce at the prevailing retail prices, you can sometimes

Support your local farmers, markets.

negotiate discounts for bulk purchases. Fruits and vegetables can then be dried, or canned, for later.

Also consider buying direct from farmers for nuts and dried fruits, which you ought to consider as part of your storage system.

NEIGHBORHOOD FOOD EXCHANGE

If you live in an urban or suburban neighborhood, chances are you don't even know your neighbors. That is too bad. Find ways to get to know your neighbors. In most neighborhoods, there are people in need, while fruit from someone else goes unused. A family can only eat so many lemons, for example. Think of your neighborhood as your extended family. Your ability to work together can really make your neighborhood a pleasant, sustainable place to live. For food, if you suddenly couldn't go to the stores, you will be relying upon whatever everyone has stored, and whatever resources are growing in the backyards or neighborhood gardens. Backyard food resources, of course, depend upon the part of the country, and the season, but these resources can still be significant.

Where I live in southern California, there are typically large volumes of fruit such as loquats, citrus trees, avocadoes, carob pods, Eugenia berries, apricots, plums, and all manner of green edibles that simply drop to the ground and are never used for food. This is largely due to ignorance, and also due to the fact that when we live in a country with so many resources, we tend to overlook, ignore, and simply not see what is right underfoot. Another problem is that too many of us do not interact with our neighbors. The Neighborhood Watch meetings provide a great opportunity to do regular food exchanges.

WILD PLANTS

We strongly encourage you to learn the basic dozen or so wild foods that can be found worldwide in most environments. We urge you to find a local teacher and go on nature walks in your area and learn to accurately identify and use the foods that are already growing there.

Just think: if you have a garden, at least half of what is normally pulled up and discarded as "weeds" is actually good food. By learning about edible weeds, you are effectively doubling the output of your garden.

"SECRET" FOR DOUBLING THE FOOD FROM YOUR GARDEN:

EAT the edible weeds!

STORING FOOD

Canned goods last for years, without refrigeration, and you should allocate a special place in your garage or cupboard for as much as you need.

It can be a good idea to buy large cans in bulk for long-term storage, though you should always carefully consider your situation. For example, in large families, or at camps, large cans of food get used up quickly, and refrigeration is not a problem. We have heard from some folks who have told us they purchased large cans because that is what they thought they should do, but when they finally opened the can for a household of two, they found that it took them a very long time to eat it all. In such cases, small families are much better off with smaller containers.

To save money, you can buy bulk bags of beans, seeds, nuts, dried fruit, and such things as flour, powdered milk, powdered eggs, and so on. When you pack these for storage, you are chiefly concerned with preventing mice and rats from getting into the containers, and you want to prevent the growth of any insects inside the containers. There are numerous ways to accomplish this.

Select a cool spot in your home for your food storage. Ideally, this is a cellar, but this all depends on your particular situation. You may have to settle for a closet, or garage.

When we have purchased large bags of grains or seeds, we have packed them into plastic buckets with tight-fitting lids. The buckets were purchased, or obtained for free, from bakeries around town. Typically, we had to clean the buckets of syrup or dough, and we had to select only those buckets whose lids made a tight seal.

You can purchase such buckets at numerous food storage companies and survival stores, though you can do just as well with second-hand buckets.

With grains and seeds, we usually pour those directly into a clean bucket. You could also line the bucket first with a brown paper bag. Years ago, we would carefully place a piece of dry ice into the square. Then, we gently placed the lid on the bucket, and allowed the dry ice to evaporate, as the gas sinks into the bucket and replaces the oxygen. After an hour or so, we snapped the lid down tight, and we were done. We also use this procedure with pasta and spaghetti products.

However, today we simply buy little desiccant packages (the ones I use are "Performance Dry" purchased from www.Survivalresources. com) and add several to each bucket of stored food.

We have stored food in old metal ammo cans, which seal very tightly. Foods store well in these old metal containers, and rats cannot eat into them. On the other hand, they are heavy and not as readily available as hard plastic containers.

We have also stored food in one-gallon glass or plastic jars. Usually, these have screw-on lids. We look for the jars whose lids have a plastic seal, and then we store the jar in a cupboard where it is dark.

If you are serious about storing food and using your stored food, we strongly recommend that you obtain a good book. There are many out there. One is *LDS Preparedness Manual, V8, 2012*, by Christopher M. Parrett.

DRYING

Drying your own fruits and vegetables is not that difficult, and it's cheaper to do it yourself than to buy already dried fruits and vegetables. We have a small electric model dehydrator and we are frequently drying something. We have dried bananas, persimmons, cranberries, deer meat, squirrel meat, apples, pears, wild herbs, watercress, mushrooms, and so on. Then we just pack the dried food in a quart jar, add desiccant packages, tightly seal the jar, and store in on a shelf. Obviously, if you don't have electricity, or if you choose to not use it, you aren't going to use an electric dryer.

We also have a multi-tiered dryer composed of circular web material, which hangs in our dark garage. Foods dry quickly from above and below from the breeze. We use this for some seeds, herbs, and greens, but generally not for anything that might attract ants.

People have dried their food for millennia. In fact, perhaps the two primary methods of food storage over the centuries have been drying and pickling.

Food left in the sun, and protected from insects, will dry naturally. A few centuries ago, people then had to store their dried food in ceramic vessels, in animal skins, possibly in woven containers. Today,

This mesh dryer is excellent for many greens and herbs. Here, it is being used to dry nettle greens.

we have a broad array of glass, metal, and plastic containers that render our food insect- and rodent-proof (more or less). Many of these containers are containers that stored some other food products; once used up and washed out, the container is completely acceptable for dried food storage.

A friend of ours who grew up in Appalachia tells us that his family dried all the summer fruit that they did not can. They took the screens off the farm house, sliced the various fruits, and set the screens out in the sun. They put sheets or cheesecloth over the fruit to keep the flies from landing on the fruit.

Learn to dry your own foods. It is not difficult to do, and you will find that even if you dry just a few things, it will supplement your overall food supply.

You might also learn to can your own foods, though that is beyond the scope of this publication. There are many good cookbooks which teach you how to can, such as Skyhorse's *The Complete Book of Home Canning* or Rodale's *Stocking Up*. However, we know how hard it is to learn something new from a book, so if you have the opportunity, work alongside someone who already knows how to can. This is always the best way to learn something new.

PRESERVING PRODUCE WITH THE ZEER POT
The African Pot in Pot Device
Mohammed Bah Abba is a Nigerian potter who found a way to keep greens and vegetables fresh longer in an area where there was no electricity.

His "invention" (this idea has apparently been around for thousands of years) utilized the natural principle of evaporation. He simply made an unglazed pot that fit into a larger pot, and the space between the pots was filled with sand and then water. Vegetables were kept in the inner pot and covered with a lid.

People in his village found that vegetables stored this way kept up to a week longer than vegetables just kept in a covered pot. Though a remarkably simple invention, Abban won an award from *Time* magazine for one of the best inventions of 2001, and was awarded a $75,000 Rolex Award for Enterprise.

This is not a universal substitute for electrical refrigeration, and it certainly has its limits.

The inside temperature of the inside pot, and the length of time it can keep foods preserved, depends on many factors such as humidity, size of pot, wind, etc. But here is one example from a British student's experiments that were posted online. In order to keep a temperature of 43°F. (6°C.), the following conditions must be met:

Conditions under which an evaporative refrigerator could reach 6°C (43°F)	
Outside Temperature	**Relative Humidity**
20.5°C (69°F)	0%
18.3°C (65°F)	10%
15.3°C (59°F)	20%
13.3°C (56°F)	30%
12.2°C (54°F)	40%
10.5°C (51°F)	50%

PICKLING

Pickling that doesn't require refrigeration is akin to canning, and to do this right, you need to consult a proper cookbook. I recommend Pascal Baudar's *Wildcrafted Fermentation: Exploring, Transforming, and Preserving the Wild Flavors of Your Local Terroir* (Chelsea Green, 2020). I also like *Asian Pickles: Sweet, Sour, Salty, Cured, and Fermented Preserves* by Karen Solomon (Ten Speed Press, 2014).

Onions kept cool with the zeer pot.

Abban with his double-pot system of keeping foods cool.

Dude McLean demonstrates how to make a zeer pot at a Dirttime.com event.

We have also done quite a bit of "refrigerator pickling" of local foods. If the power went out, such foods might last a while, but would spoil if not heavily salted.

MAKING WILD PICKLES

We have gained a new appreciation for many of our "wild greens" ever since we began to make pickles from the young flower buds.

Since food storage and preservation is nearly a lost art, many of the methods of pickling are long forgotten. Refrigeration and supermarkets have made it easy to rely on commercially prepared foods. Having learned a few pickling methods, we know that there will always be a place for the simple skills of living off the land, whether in the urban or rural setting.

In our area here in the suburbs of Los Angeles, the open fields fill up every spring with sow thistle, mallow, and wild radish, all common and ubiquitous "weeds" that are commonly found nationwide. We have used these plants in our soups and salads for over four decades, and have always enjoyed learning new methods of preparation.

During a visit to a friend's home, he insisted that we all try some of his homemade "pickles." These were not pickled cucumbers, and the aroma when he opened the jar was strong and robust. We each tried a spoonful of the little pickles, or "capers." He had used the young flower buds of the sow thistle.

We were excited by the prospect of another food item from a wild plant with which we were already familiar. Our friend told us that he simply packs the washed sow thistle buds into glass jars, fills them with raw apple cider vinegar, and puts them into the refrigerator. He lets the buds steep in the vinegar for at least a month before he starts eating them. He told us that the ones we sampled were over a year old.

This, of course, is not what is meant by "canning," where refrigeration is not needed. This was simply an easy method to create refrigerated pickles. Our friend told us that besides raw apple cider vinegar, he has also used the left-over liquid from a jar of commercial pickles, or olives, or from pickled jalapeños.

We were eager to try this simple method: it meant we'd be able to harvest more from our wild orchard and extend our food supply.

We picked at least four different plants to use for our wild pickles or "capers." We used the young flower buds of the sow thistle.

The mallow plant, also called cheeseweed, is also a source of "capers." After the plant flowers, the fruit that forms is round and flat.

These are good if you get them while they are still green and have not matured into dry seeds yet.

The wild radish plant is in the mustard family, and the flower formula is identical to the wild mustards. However, the wild radish flower is lavender fading to white, and the leaves are tastier and spicier than most mustards. Also, one uniqueness of the wild radish is the plump seed pod that develops after the flowers mature. These pods somewhat resemble jalapeño peppers and are good for pickles. We have pickled these in the past, and served them to guests who thought they were some sort of serrano or jalapeño pepper.

Lastly, we have nasturtium growing all over the orchard areas. Nasturtium grows wild along the West Coast beaches and it sprawls all over an area with rich soil and some shade. It is very common in our orchard area. We pick the new flower buds and the two-lobed fruit. We have to get the fruit while it is still green and tender, not when it has hardened.

The simple procedure is to first rinse all the buds, flowers, or fruits. This is best done by putting all the to-be-picked material into a bowl and adding lukewarm water. This loosens any insects and dirt and allows you to pick out any less-than-perfect buds, pods, etc. Then rinse them in a colander, and put them into glass jars. Cover with raw apple cider vinegar, close the lid, and put the jar into the refrigerator. That's all there is to it! You can add raw honey, garlic cloves, cayenne, kelp, and a pinch of sea salt.

Though we eat some of these immediately, they improve as they age. Ideally, you should let them sit for about two months before you start using them.

FOOD STORAGE COMPANIES

Sometimes, it is worthwhile to make a big purchase at once and get a year's supply of certain items. Once again, we recommend that you look for specials, and even ask for a discount if none is offered.

We have purchased many perfectly good #10 cans of all sorts of food items from yard sales. In one case, it was a divorce sale, and we paid $50 for what would have cost over $700 when new. Some of the canned goods were not things we would ordinarily eat, and some of the grain was old and rancid, but our chickens loved it. Still, we feel the $50 was well worth it.

By the way, in that instance the man knew the cans were worth much more than the $50 we offered, and we only offered $50 because that's all we wanted to pay, and we were okay if he said "no." However, he only agreed to the deal when we agreed to also buy a book shelf for $10.

BACKPACKING FREEZE-DRIED FOOD

Though some of this is quite good, we find that it is almost all over-priced. Therefore, we would not recommend obtaining your food storage supplies from backpacking stores, unless it is a year-end special, a close-out, or other sale at significantly reduced prices.

MREs

Then there is the military food in retort packages. MRE means Meal Ready to Eat. But some folks say that MRE really means Meals Rejected by Ethiopians, a phrase apparently based on a real incident. The contract for making MREs, we are told, goes to the lowest bidder, which should tell you something about their relative quality.

Still, you might consider having some MREs in your storage. Read the ingredients, as some are better than others. There is a shelf life of around ten years, and you can actually just drop the pouches into boiling water and they are ready to eat. I have laid an MRE pouch on a hot rock in the summer and the contents were hot in thirty minutes. Since the contents are already cooked, you could also eat one right out of the package if necessary.

If you use these, we recommend using them as part of a balanced meal, and adding fresh greens and other food items to them. MREs can be a good part of your food storage if you feel that the ingredients are acceptable to you, and if you can get significant discounts by buying a box at a time.

RAISING ANIMALS

Since there are entire books already out there on how to raise animals for the backyard or homestead, we won't be going into this topic in detail.

However, in my backyard in Los Angeles, I raised many chickens, rabbits, a goose, had a pet pig, and raised bees. These are the easiest (and most quiet) for the urban setting.

Though I was largely a vegetarian and didn't eat any of my animals, I enjoyed the daily fresh eggs from the chickens. These were the best eggs I have ever eaten!

I built their coop, which was about eight by twenty feet, and big enough to walk into. They had perches, and their nesting boxes were recycled five-gallon plastic nursery pots which were mounted horizontally to the wall, about a foot off the ground.

The bees were kept in a semi-wooded area of the back where they could fly away all day into the nearby eucalyptus orchard. I harvested

Many people keep chickens these days, even in the city.

Where the conditions are right, bees can be kept in the city.

the honey when needed, and the honey was as dark as molasses from the eucalyptus flowers, and was truly medicinal.

SUMMARY OF FOOD STORAGE METHODS

METHOD	COMMENT
MREs ("meals ready to eat" / food in retort pouches)	These are pre-cooked, can be eaten without warming. They already have water. Often too salty. Can be diluted.
Canned foods	Require no refrigeration, and you can get just about anything in a can. For information on the shelf life of canned goods, go to www.usda.gov.
Home canning	Great way to store backyard produce. Will last two to three years without refrigeration.
Dried foods (herbs, seeds, grains, vegetables, etc.)	The universal way that food was prepared for storage in pre-electrical days. Shelf life varies depending on the item. Wheat, for example, lasts hundreds of years if stored properly.

METHOD	COMMENT
Pickled food: with vinegar	You can make pickled foods to refrigerate or not refrigerate, and this is easy to do.
Salt "pickled"	Salted foods can last a long time, within reason. Usually, salted foods need to be rinsed before eating.
The refrigerator!	Obviously, this appliance was invented to store food and keep it fresh longer than without it. Everyone in the city regards it as an essential expense. Many are highly efficient, but most are not. The main downside is that they must have electricity, though this can be supplied with the sun.

SUMMARY

There are many reasons to store food, and to raise food on your premises. You do not have to be worrying about the rapid collapse of Western civilization to have good reasons to store food. Remember, "storing food" doesn't have to mean a garage full of canned goods. But it does mean having more than one day's supply of food at your home. This saves you trips to the store, and it's actually more economical to buy food in bulk.

I have some friends who choose to not have a refrigerator due to the fact that it is one of the most inefficient energy hogs of the modern household. Granted, most of us *want* that refrigerator because, inefficient as it is, it allows us to keep food longer.

One of these friends told me that she preferred to not be "hooked up to" the refrigerator, and not having one not only significantly lowered her monthly electric bill, but it also made her think about her food-buying choices much more carefully. Yes, she purchased canned goods, dried pasta, pickled foods, and many other dry goods that did not need refrigeration. In addition, she created her own little evaporative cooler in which she kept the few perishables that she did purchase. Plus, in her case, she lived only a short five-minute walk to a local store where she could purchase perishable goods. So this worked in her case, though it might not work in every case.

My sensei Barton Boehm told me that when he was doing his initial martial arts training in Japan, he lived in the small town of Oppama. This was a very poor neighborhood. Each small house (a large room, really) had one electric light. There was no such thing as air conditioning. The "heating" was a small hibachi that burned charcoal or wood. The toilet was the public binjo a block away. And there was no such thing as a refrigerator in every home. Fortunately for this small town, one could purchase fresh vegetables, mushrooms, sprouts, and tofu either in the local market, or from the vendors who came by in bicycles. In fact, the people of Oppama were living a very ecological lifestyle, though not necessarily by choice. Rather, they lived this way because of economic poverty. Eventually, the government of Japan tore down that entire poor section and built more modern apartments for the residents to live in.

WHAT DID I LEARN?

1. List three possible food sources from your own urban property.
2. List three ways to store food if you have no electricity, and therefore no working refrigerator.
3. List at least three "ornamental" plants that you can grow on your property that also produce a food.

CHAPTER FIVE

COOKING: MAKING MEALS WITH ALTERNATE FUELS

Gas and electric ranges are certainly convenient. But what if you want to cook your food by a "sustainable" method? What are your options?

BARBEQUE, HIBACHI, FIREPIT

Many of you have backyard barbeques and hibachis. Your problems are over. That's how you'll cook your food, and all you need to do is ensure a supply of firewood.

We have formed a simple circle of cinder blocks out on our brick patio, and use it for building fires. By placing a grill over this fire, we are able to cook soup, stews, eggs, potatoes, anything! Anyone who has ever built a campfire already knows how to do this.

Begin with a safe surface. We do it on our brick patio because we know it is safe there and the fire cannot spread. The circle of cinder blocks creates a fire ring about three feet in diameter. It could be smaller, or larger, in your yard, depending on your needs. Then we build our fire, and place a simple grill over the flames. This is the simplest of all emergency cooking methods. It requires only an open safe place to make the fire, fuel, a grill, and someone at least as intelligent as a tenderfoot Boy Scout.

BACKPACKING STOVES

If you go backpacking or car camping, you probably already have a great stove that is portable, compact, and runs on propane, kerosene, or white gas. You could use this in your backyard if there was no natural gas coming into your home. Many backpacking-style stoves could be safely used in apartments as well.

The key factor in emergency planning with such a stove is to be certain you have adequate fuel.

NEWSPAPER LOGS: RECYCLING NEWSPAPERS INTO BURNABLE "LOGS"

In the genuine wilderness, firewood is everywhere, and abundant. Well, more or less. But if you're trying to be self-sufficient in the city, and you want to provide your own fuel, you might be able to cook your meals with wood prunings from your yard. Maybe.

In today's urban setting, there are many resources that are common, even abundant. One such resource that could be pressed into service in an emergency is newspaper. (Though, come to think of it, in another few years newspapers might go the way of the Dodo bird.)

Newspaper, obviously, can be used for many things, such as wrapping, making pots for your garden, emergency insulation, and also for making logs for the fireplace.

When I say "logs," I'm not referring to the old 1970s method of rolling some newspaper around a broom handle, tying it up, pulling out the handle, and then burning the "log" like a wooden log. Trouble is, these don't really burn all that well unless you already have a blazing fire going.

But there is an alternative. Put all your newspapers into a plastic bucket and add water. Soaking it for a few days is best. On occasion, when I have demonstrated this to children at camp, we simply shredded the newspaper, added water, and went to the next step, but soaking for a few days is ideal.

Next, you need to have a newspaper press, as pictured. I first purchased one around 1980, and though this model doesn't seem to be available anymore, there are similar ones today manufactured by others

The newspaper "mush" is placed into the rectangular box.

y Hartman with bucket of soaked
wspapers, and a unique press
hich makes burnable "bricks" from
wspapers.

e two handles of the lid of the
ss are used to press down on the
wspaper mush, which squeezes out
ch of the water.

which seems to work just as well. (Look for these products on Amazon.)

You put the wet newspaper into the rectangular box section of the press, add the top, and then push the handles down to press out the water. You then pop out the "brick" and let it dry for a few days (or longer). It then burns well in a fireplace or campfire. Granted, this is newspaper, so don't expect the same BTU of oak or other hard woods. But it does burn, and is definitely better than the logs rolled around a broomstick. I've used them in backyard campfires and in woodstoves.

This device also presents the possibility for dealing with security documents. If you just toss your paper documents into the city trash can or the city recycling bin, you never really know what might happen. I used to just burn such documents on a grill in the backyard, but this is not always a possibility. The last time I had a

Jay Hartman finishes pressing out the water from the newspaper brick.

Jay Hartman shows the wet newspaper brick he just pressed.

Wet newspaper bricks must be set out to dry. After about two weeks, they will be completely dry and can be burned.

The newspaper press, and two dry newspaper bricks which are now ready for burning.

full bag of documents to deal with—old bills, etc.—I shredded them and put them into a bucket with water. Since they are mostly bond paper, not newsprint, I allowed a week of soaking. After the week, I made some logs and dried them. Since you can no longer read anything on the bills and documents after this, there is no need to burn them right away. And since bills are typically bond paper, the logs seem to burn just a bit hotter and longer.

I realize that not every home has a fireplace, and residents of southern California are not likely to freeze to death, such as Polish and German people did during WWII in that more-northern locale. But you could still use these "logs" to cook food or heat water over a backyard grill.

FOOTNOTE

Don't have enough newspaper for your cooking needs? Well, you all know what I think about eucalyptus trees, right? Cut them down, let them dry, and you'll have years of firewood.

SOLAR COOKING FOR FREE

Low-cost, efficient solar cookers you can make in an afternoon

By now, we've all heard about solar cookers of one sort or another. And you know an idea has finally gone "mainstream" when you open a glossy mail-order catalog and find solar cookers for sale. Nevertheless, most residents of the United States still think of solar cookers as some sort of novelty, perhaps a good weekend project for Scouts but not something that is practical and useful. This viewpoint is unfortunate. In part, this attitude results from the high cost of pre-fab solar cookers—some cost several hundred dollars! Plus many people believe that their yard doesn't get enough sun to make solar cookers practical.

In fact, solar cookers are practical in every state of the Union (except Alaska) for at least six to eight months every year. As for cost, you could purchase a pre-fab solar cooker used, or on sale if the full retail price is too much. You could also make one.

Many readers of *Mother Earth News* have made their own solar cookers described in past issues, particularly the parabolic dish solar cooker, and the "bread box" design made from wood or sheet metal.

BOX-IN-A-BOX DESIGN

A simple solar cooker can be made with cardboard boxes.

First, get two cardboard boxes. One should be able to fit into the other, with ideally an inch space all around. (If you can't find boxes, you can cut and tape your own boxes from cardboard.) Now, cover the inside of the little box with aluminum foil, and make sure that you tape down any loose flaps on either box.

All the supplies you need to make this simple solar cooker: two boxes (one must be able to fit into the other), aluminum foil, newspaper, duct tape, a piece of glass.

Now, placing the little box into the bigger box, the tops of each box should be at the same level. To accomplish this you need to support the inner box so that it is off the floor of the bigger box. This is done by placing small pieces of flat wood or cardboard inside the big box. Generally, four small pieces of wood will serve as four "legs" to support the inner box.

Line the inside of the smaller box with aluminum foil.

Once you've placed and glued these four "legs," you pack all the space between the two boxes with crumpled newspapers. Though most people have no problem obtaining old newspapers for the required insulation, you can use many other substances for insulation: old cotton rags, straw, dried grass, coconut fibres, etc. Though you might be tempted to use those white blown-foam packing chips for insulation, DON'T! At high temperatures, they may melt and/or give off undesirable fumes.

Now that you have one box inside another, with both of their tops level, and with the insulation packed between the boxes, you are ready to seal the insulation. This is done simply by taping (or gluing pieces of cardboard) over the top open section between the two boxes. I generally just use duct tape.

Insert the smaller box into the larger box. Pack the space between the boxes with crushed newspaper. Make sure to insulate the space at the bottom.

Next, make a lid for your cooker. If you were lucky enough to find a large cardboard box with a tight fitting lid, you can now proceed with that lid. However, you may need to cut a lid from cardboard. To do this, measure the size of the big box, and then cut your cardboard at least one inch larger on all sides. This is so you can fold down the edges and have a flap to your lid.

Once you have made your secure-fitting lid, you are ready to cut an opening for a sheet of glass or a heavy-duty sheet of plastic.

Up to this point, you could have constructed everything from old boxes and from supplies you have around the house.

You now want to cut an opening in the lid that is just as big as the opening of the inner box. Save the piece of cardboard that you cut out, since you can use it later as a reflector.

Tape the space between the two boxes. Then make the lid with a piece of glass.

The opening of the lid will need to be covered with a single pane of glass, or with a sheet of plastic. Plastic might be easier to obtain, but glass will retain the heat better. The glass or plastic must be secured to the top of the lid by glue, or silicone caulking, or duct tape. Make certain that the glass is secure before proceeding.

Now, let's make a reflector from the flap that you cut out of the lid. Line the inside of this lid flap with aluminum foil, and you have a reflector. Tape it next to the window on the lid. When the solar cooker is in use, you prop up the reflector with a stick.

Presto! Your solar cooker is complete! Remove the lid, and add food items to the inside. Prop up the box so that the glass faces the sun. Keep your food items smaller for faster cooking.

A few comments:

The finished solar box cooker. The flap covered in aluminum foil can be adjusted to shine more sunlight into the box. When not in use, the flap protects the glass.

By carefully planning before you begin the actual work, you will produce a quality cooker at minimal effort. For example, rather than rotely follow any dimensions we have provided here, first see what sort of supplies you have at hand. You may have a good pane of glass, and so you should adjust the cooker's size based upon the glass. Or you may find two ideal cardboard boxes, and so you adjust all sizes accordingly.

Before you cook, you should place a black metal cookie tray, or an aluminum foil trail, on the inside of the cooker.

Of course, using the solar cooker is easy. To absorb the heat, all cooking pots should be black, and should be covered. Food items cook faster if they are in smaller pieces. You should always allow twice as much cooking time in a solar cooker. The solar cooker is one of the simplest ways to cook, and it forces you to plan your meals in advance.

COMMERCIAL SOLAR COOKERS

THE SUN OVEN: This is a commercially manufactured solar oven that traps the sun's heat. It is a significant improvement over the box cooker that you make with scrap cardboard. On a sunny day, the Sun Oven cooks about as fast as cooking on a gas stove. I have used one for over twenty years and really enjoy it!

Actor Ed Begley Jr. with the Sun Oven that he uses in his yard.

THE SOLSOURCE

SolSource manufactures quality parabolic disc solar cookers. These look like the old dishes for cable TV. They are lightweight and easy to assemble. They sit on the ground, and are pointed at the sun. A sturdy mount allows you to cook foods, and on a hot day, these cook as quickly as foods cooked on a gas stove.

In fact, we have placed a piece of paper into the focal point of this cooker and the paper burst into flame in about a minute, meaning that temperatures in excess of 400°F were achieved.

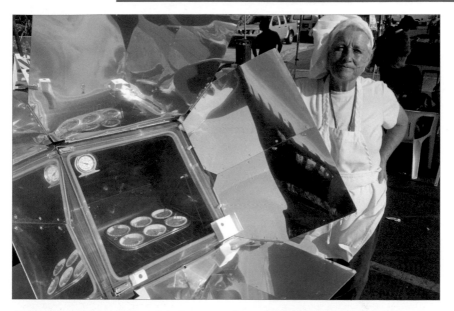

Chef Prudence Boczarski publicly demonstrating the viability of the Sun Oven at a farmers' market.

A man feels the heat radiating from the Sun Oven.

The internal thermostat lets you know your cooking temperature.

Using the SolSource dish cooker.

Cooking an egg dish with the SolSource parabolic dish cooker.

I love this cooker, and it's an ideal way to cook your food. Even if all your appliances are working, this is a great way to cook outside without flames during the heat of the summer.

WOODSTOVES/WOOD FIREPLACES

If you have already installed a woodstove, or a fireplace, you have the ability to cook your food and warm your home, providing you have a supply of fuel. If you have trees or bushes in your yard, you should be able to provide at least some of your fuel from your prunings that have dried.

At flea markets and yard sales, I have actually purchased three different wood-burning stoves at bargain prices over the years. But for various reasons, none was quite right. In our home, we just wanted a well-built workhorse that would cook our food and/or warm the house.

Finally, my wife, Dolores, found a free-standing fireplace at a yard sale, and we purchased it for $70. In fact, though there are plenty of places that sell top-notch new woodstoves and fireplaces; we have seen used woodstoves and fireplaces on sale many times. You don't need to be any sort of expert to determine if the used one is worth buying or not—just examine it top to bottom, inside and outside, for breaks, deep rust, burned-out sections, parts not connected well. Shake it to see if it all holds together, and of course, it has to be of a style and design to fit both your needs and your home.

One of our great surprises was how much all the piping costs to actually install the stove *safely* in your home. A fireplace shop originally quoted me $700 for all the piping we needed from the wood fireplace to the spark arrester at the top. After many phone calls and queries, I ended up paying less than half that from a company that supplies hardware stores. Be sure to shop around and ask questions.

So Dolores found a great wood fireplace, and I got a bargain on the piping. And then everything sat in our garage for nearly a year before I installed it. I spent far more time thinking about the details of the project than it actually took to do the real work. Though I had never installed a stove pipe before, by asking enough questions, I was able to get the entire project finished in about three hours. Granted, everyone's situation will be a bit different, but if you ask lots of questions, shop around, and take your time when you do the actual installation, you are likely to be very satisfied.

A view of the simple sheet metal woodstove that the author installed in his home. The bend in the vent allowed for more heat in the room.

The wood fireplace has a small flat top, not really large enough for any serious cooking. I have heated some drinks and other small things on the top, but it is really used for heating the house. We were amazed at how well the fireplace heated most of the house—not just the living room—with just a few logs. We remembered that with built-in fireplaces, they never heated the room that well. We concluded that this free-standing wood fireplace did a better job for several reasons: 1) It set out in the room about two feet; 2) as a corner model, the heat radiated outward to the entire room; and 3) there was the added heating from the five or six feet of piping inside the room.

Our wood fireplace has completely transformed our home. We would strongly encourage anyone without one to seriously consider installing one. Though we had not been heating with gas, we had been (on very cold nights) using those small electric heaters that really drive up the electric bill. The wood fireplace made the home really feel like a home. It became the "heart" of the house, and we now are uncertain how we got along without it.

Also, we have plenty of firewood readily available, and so that made the fuel easy. We were actually doing a neighbor a favor by cleaning up and removing large volumes of dead and fallen wood on his property.

It is easy to see why a wood fireplace and/or woodstove are virtually synonymous with self-reliance and homestead living. There, all wrapped in one, you have a heater, a cooker, and the "caveman TV." If you can stay warm without having to pay exorbitant fuel costs, you're on your way to self-reliance. And if you can cook your food without gas or electricity, well, you are really on the right track. Plus, if we have sensitive papers that we don't want to just toss out into the city's recycling bins (who knows who may see them?), we simply use them as tinder for the evening's fire.

A word of warning: Homes burn down all the time, either from gas explosions, from fireplaces, woodstoves, Christmas trees, etc. Don't cut any corners when it comes to installing your stove or fireplace safely. You want to stay safely warm *inside* your home; you don't want to be outside, watching the house go up in flames because you tried to save a few dollars somewhere.

Go into this with a determination to do an impeccable job, and your woodstove or fireplace will be a rewarding part of your urban or rural homestead.

CHAPTER SIX

GENERAL HYGIENE: TOILET, BATHING, WASHING, SOAPS, ET AL.

If you live in a water-rich environment, the availability of water for all your needs may not be much of an issue. But if you've chosen to personally be a wiser user of your resources, you should find more and more ways to use water wisely.

Piped water is convenient, obviously. But if you chose to live remotely, or nomadically, or if drought befalls your community and you want to stay, you have no choice but to find ways to use less, use it more efficiently, and recycle it. But we also want to keep the pores of our body open and "breathing," all the while getting the most mileage out of that water. Here are some ideas.

SHOWER VS. BATHTUB

I've often heard it said that a shower is more efficient than a bath. Is that a fact? The amount of water used with either a shower or a bath is entirely a factor of how long the person stands in the shower, or how full you fill the tub. One is not inherently more efficient than the other, as far as water use is concerned.

A quick shower can certainly use less water than a bath, but I've also taken baths with very little water.

Here are my reasons why I believe that a bath is more efficient overall.

1. Bath water can be bottled and used to flush the toilet, water the plants, even wash the dog.
2. Each bather can wash three or four articles of personal clothing during each bath, thereby reducing weekly wash loads. For this reason, we recommend using environmentally safe detergents in your bath water. Basic H has been our top recommendation for years, though the price is ridiculous. This biodegradable liquid detergent leaves your bathtub without a ring, and its pH balance leaves your skin without a soapy film. (Today, there are plenty of environmentally safe liquid detergents available, including Ivory's dishwashing liquid.)
3. A small amount of bath oil (or olive oil, and/or fresh lemon peel) and bath salts turn the plain old tub into a luxury spa of health-giving qualities that a shower can't begin to match.

By the time one steps out of even a steaming hot shower, the body has barely begun to sweat. Instead of continuing this healthful poison-eliminating process, the body is quickly wiped dry and talcum powder and after-shower powder and antiperspirants are lathered onto the body, which instantly plugs the perspiration ducts. This effectively seals the poisons into our bodies so we can "look good" and "smell good." Then we scurry to join the others on the nerve-shattering freeways for the purpose of rushing to those places where we will focus eight to twelve hours "making money." But then... that's another story... This daily cleansing should not be rushed.

Every body pore is an excretory organ. A quick shower cannot possibly cleanse these tiny pores that are so vital to our health. But an hour-long submersion in hot water does the job magnificently. A stiff bristle brush is recommended for scrubbing the entire body once the perspiration has begun to flow. This simple scrubbing provides the TRUE "deep-cleaning" that many commercial beauty preparations claim but cannot deliver. The hardest scrubbing should be focused on the bottom of the feet, the hands, buttocks, and neck. The scalp (not the hair) must be thoroughly scrubbed as well.

A BRUSH BATH

Incidentally, a stiff brush can give an excellent "air bath" if no water is available (e.g., on a camping trip, or when you are just practicing getting more with less). If you are unable to bathe, it is crucial to use this technique to keep your pores open and "discharging." A vigorous dry brushing over the entire body will leave you feeling (almost) as if you'd just come out of a bath.

I used to find a dry brush bath uncomfortable, bordering on painful. The brush can't be too soft or it will have no effect. But it can't be too tough either, because it could damage your skin. You have to experiment to find one that is just right for you. After much experimentation, I found that a brush manufactured by the Fuller Brush Company, called the "golden triangle," was the best stiffness for my skin. Even when I am taking a regular bath or shower, I prefer to go over the entire surface of my body and scrub the skin without water. It feels a bit as if I've had a massage, and I don't feel really complete unless I do this. The dry brushing probably removes many more dead skin cells than are removed when the skin is wet and more flexible, though I'm not really sure about that.

RECYCLING THE TUB WATER

To be the most efficient user of water resources, you use only what you need, and you make every attempt to recycle your used household water back into your yard, to water your trees and garden.

To recycle your tub water without changing your drain pipe, you can use half-gallon or gallon plastic containers. If you stay in the bathtub a long time, you'll need to periodically regulate both the water temperature and rising water level. Rather than pull the drain, fill up these plastic containers with water and set them outside the tub. These containers of water can be recycled later by using them to flush the toilet (more on that in a moment).

Besides the tub water that we've stored in the plastic containers, there's another way to recycle bath water. This is where you re-route your pipe so the tub drain goes out into your yard. You can do this by yourself, with the aid of a few good books, plus the cooperation of a knowledgeable plumber. Go under your house, disconnect the pipe that goes from your tub to the city sewer system. This will usually be one-and-a-half-inch-diameter pipe. Next, screw the appropriate lengths of one-and-a-half- to two-inch pipe onto your bathtub drain so that the water goes out to your garden or fruit trees. If you first draw a schematic diagram, then measure everything accurately before you start, it can be an amazingly simple job. Those who live on a second story can run their pipe over to the second story wall, then attach a hose which runs down to the garden.

The biggest expense—the pipe—can often be purchased used. Any needed threading (if not already threaded) can be done at the local hardware store, or you can rent a threading tool.

Also consider: if you do the job in PVC, you'll likely be doing some of the fastening with glue. The cost of PVC is less, although the lifespan may be shorter than galvanized pipe, especially if any part is exposed to sunlight.

Two things to remember: 1) Be sure to plan the new drain pipe so that there is a continuous slight downward sloping until it reaches your garden. Flat spots will slow the water flow, causing a gradual buildup of solids that will eventually clog the pipe; 2) Be sure that you bathe exclusively with biodegradable detergents. Soaps and other chemicalized cleansers may even kill your plants. There are many bio-degradable detergents. We have long recommended Basic H, but due to its unreasonably high cost, you might consider Dawn Free, Ivory dish washing liquid, and several other lesser-known products.

Oh, there is a third issue too—the various zoning and building regulations of cities. Though city officials often "talk green," it's often another story when the building and safety department comes out and tells you that you cannot do grey-water recycling without expensive permits, storage containers, pumps, et al. I know there is a reason why we have these urban regulations, but sometimes they simply make it impossible to do what is really a very simple procedure. There are also issues with neighborhood associations. So, do your research and plan your system well so that it doesn't cause neighbors to complain.

A SOLAR SHOWER

Everyone should have a device for taking a solar shower. I carry one with me whenever I go camping. In fact, before these were so widely available, I created one using a heavy-duty plastic bag to which we attached a plastic spigot that I purchased in the household section of some store.

I've used them when my main line to my home was being repaired, and I had to use my stored water for a while.

You fill the container with water and lay it in the sun. Then, hang it in a tree and take a hot shower! Easy! Lay it out in the sun early in the day to make sure you get it hot enough. In fact, in the summer, the water gets so hot that I have to just let the water trickle out a little at a time.

If you have a large family, you should get a few of these.

Note: These solar showers come in various sizes, from one to five gallons. The small gallon

Rick Adams shows one example of a commercial solar shower. This Sun Shower model is 2 ½ gallons.

sizes are great for single backpackers, and on a hot day, a gallon heats up quickly. However, the five-gallon size weighs over forty pounds when full of water, and it's often hard to find a tree branch that will safely hold so many pounds of water. I recommend the two-and-a-half-gallon size for both overall efficiency and weight consideration.

Also, when you check at camping stores where this is sold, they also make a simple breakdown "closet" that you can use for privacy when taking your shower, and this is well worth having even in your own backyard.

THE TOILET

Remember, you can flush your toilet even if the incoming water line is not working. This may be surprising, but it's true—as long as the sewer pipe is not clogged nor broken.

The water tank behind (or above) the bowl is just a water reservoir that is kept filled by the incoming city water. Its function is to release a large volume of water into the bowl (when you push the flush lever) and thereby force the bowl's contents away into the sewer. The city water then automatically refills the reservoir (that's what causes the hissing noise after each flush).

And what would happen if you turned off the city water to the reservoir? The reservoir wouldn't refill after each flush. Then, when you tried to flush the next time, nothing would happen. However, even if there is no incoming water (or if you choose to turn it off), you can still flush as long as the drain pipes are intact. Here's how:

You first take two one-gallon plastic containers with handles (such as Purex containers) and, using a sharp knife or a pair of strong scissors, cut off the entire top so you have an opening that is approximately four inches across. Try to not cut off or damage the handle. These two containers are then filled with bath water, then stashed out of sight behind the toilet. When you need to flush, pour in the water from these containers simultaneously. Believe it or not, two gallons is all you need to accomplish what the automatic toilet flush requires five gallons to do.

[Note: Even if you have one of the relatively new toilets that only require one or two gallons of water per flush, you'd still be saving water by recycling your bath water in this way.]

You then refill the two containers with water from all those other half- and one-gallon containers you filled from your bath water. Finally, to bring the toilet bowl water level back to normal, you'll need to pour in another half-gallon of your recycled bath water. If you save enough bath water, you will <u>never</u> <u>again</u> need to use clean city water to flush your toilet.

Now for those of you who are starting to worry about the prospect of your lovely bathroom becoming wall-to-wall plastic containers, fret not. A family of four, each bathing every other day, will need ten to twelve gallons of stored water, depending on the frequency of elimination. One extra shelf along a wall is more than adequate; or you can work out your own ingenious storage system depending on your particular space limitations. In one household of four adults and one child where this was done for over ten years, a shelf was built to hold eighteen containers. An additional six containers were kept between the sink and bathtub. This may sound like a lot of containers, but they really aren't in the way unless you stumble into the bathroom just after someone has taken a bath and hasn't yet had the chance to put the containers away.

The reward for this course of action might and might not be a lower water bill. However, if your motivation for such action is to be a personal part of the solution, then virtue is its own reward, and you'll have a peace of mind that comes from knowing you're doing what you can for Earth's ecology, and that you're not part of the problem.

If you don't have the space to store these containers, or if you can't or don't want to convert your plumbing to a grey-water system, you can simply carry the full containers outside after each bath and water your garden and fruit trees.

OTHER TOILET ALTERNATIVES

I had to chuckle when I read about a family who decided to shorten the length of their "survival test" because their Porta-Potti "broke."

The family wanted to see how well they'd survive in their urban home if an earthquake severed all utility lines and truck routes to the city. So they turned off their water, their gas, and their electricity and used only the food, water, candles, and other supplies they had stored in the home.

They called off their "test" when their "emergency toilet" ceased working properly. But why did they stop their "test" when it was just becoming real? After all, when a crisis is suddenly upon us, we have no time for buying an alternative toilet. You just use what is available.

The subject of human waste disposal is perhaps the most sensitive and most ignored area of disaster planning. Why? Because in our sophisticated, modern society, we don't want to bother with such things. We use the toilet, flush, and forget. Let someone else worry about it.

Yet, properly composted human excrement can be a valuable source of fertilizer and even burnable gas, as the Chinese have proven. As of the early '80s, there were 7.2 million methane digesters in rural China that use human and animal wastes to provide fuel and fertilizer for about 35 million rural people.

RV TOILET

Since Western toilets are big water users, anyone seeking a low-impact lifestyle, even in the city, eventually gets around to rethinking the toilet. Is there an alternative?

I once exclusively used a simple RV bucket toilet in my Los Angeles home for a period of three months. This was part of a testing program of the non-profit corporation with which I was affiliated. The test's purpose was to ascertain the practicality of such a toilet after an earthquake. We also just wanted to see if an inexpensive toilet could be used in the city, or in the back woods where there were no drains or cesspools.

When full, I emptied the bucket into a trench in my yard, which was then layered with straw, worms, and worm castings. Eventually, I planted tomato plants in the trench, and ate the tomatoes a few months later.

Kevin Sutherland examines a hospital potty, which can be used in the backyard for emergencies.

Conventional outhouses can be used in remote areas where there is no plumbing, and they can be easily converted into "composting toilets" by adding sawdust after each use, and doing periodic cleaning.

The simple bucket was not difficult to use. The real challenge involved finding an effective and ecological method to combat the odor. After various experiments, we found that the most practical and economical method for eliminating the "toilet odor" was adding lemon juice and baking soda into the toilet after each use.

WORM FARM

Three years later I conducted another such test, this time in my backyard. This was my "worm toilet." In a secluded, private spot, I set up an outdoor toilet. The toilet consisted of a hospital toilet seat potty, and, instead of the usual pot under the seat, I used a large wooden box. The box was of a size that fit well under the potty. Into the box I placed a layer of worms and worm castings and a bit of partially decomposed straw. After each use of this toilet, I covered the excrement with another layer of worms and worm castings. This system proved to be simple, odor-free, and fly-free. The key to its success was the addition of earthworms. I used a type of earthworm known as "redworms." Redworms are the most common worm bred in back-yard worm farms because they are rapid breeders and can tolerate a broad temperature range. Earthworms continually burrow and digest organic matter, breaking it down into nitrogen-rich plant food.

After the box under the toilet became full, I moved it to the side and gave the earthworms time to process the contents. In each case, two months was adequate for full decomposition of all excrement and toilet paper. When I added the contents of each seasoned box around the base of my fruit trees, it all appeared as a rich, loamy soil that was full of earthworms.

The idea for such a toilet came to me when observing the earth-worm farm I had established under my rabbit coop. The rabbits were in suspended cages which had a screen-mesh bottoms, allowing their droppings to fall out. Using old lumber, I created a frame on the ground under the rabbit coop. Earthworms proliferated rapidly with the regular rabbit droppings and urine, and there was a conspicuous absence of flies and odors around the farm, and it greatly reduced the necessary cleaning to the rabbit coop.

I was motivated to pursue this project for other reasons besides earthquake preparedness. Some estimates indicate that about 50 per-cent of the average urban household's water is used to flush the toi-let. Anyone who is concerned about the huge water waste in modern toilets and the waste of a potentially valuable fertilizer has no doubt investigated commercial composting toilets. But even the cheapest of such toilets costs around $1,000. Thus, I attempted to find an easier and cheaper method that would still conform to all standards of health and cleanliness, and ease of operation.

My worm toilet is still an ongoing project, and I still experiment. But the potential is obvious. Not only could such a toilet save vast amounts of water, it would be economically viable if set up properly, and it would be practical after a disaster such as an earthquake. In wilderness areas, such as national parks and at remote cabins, such a toilet makes far more sense than the current outhouse whose contents are considered "waste matter" at best, and a health hazard at worst.

COMMERCIALLY AVAILABLE ECOLOGICAL TOILETS

Composting toilets have been available commercially for at least forty years, and there are many new products to choose from. Where drought and water usage are an issue, many cities are more willing to work with homeowners who want to install a composting toilet. There are many available to choose from, and the price range starts at as low as $60 to well over a thousand dollars, depending on how high-tech of a toilet you need. You can begin your inquiries at building supply stores, and continue your research with Google and Amazon.

There are many available composting toilets. Here is one, the Sun-Mar.

Another view of the commercially available Sun-Mar composting toilet.

TOILET PAPER

We had not planned to add this short section on toilet paper, but the panic-buying of toilet paper during the coronavirus crisis of 2020 made us reconsider.

In March 2020 it was impossible to buy toilet paper from any of the big box stores and supermarkets, as toilet paper and water for some inexplicable reason became the number one item that people decided to stock up on. Toilet paper became hard to get in even the office supply stores.

To be sure, toilet paper is one of those products of modern civilization that makes life a bit easier. On the other hand, for the vast sweep of time that humans have been on the earth, we have figured out how to keep our rear ends clean after each bowel movement, using leaves or other substance.

During long camping trips, we always found ways to utilize nature for substitute toilet paper—usually large leaves such as sycamore, maple, mullein, and so on. We learned to properly use whatever was available.

My mother grew up on a farm in rural Ohio, and lived there during the Depression. In her youth, the farmhouse had no indoor plumbing and they used an outhouse. Having toilet paper was a luxury. For toilet paper, they used pieces of newspaper, and catalog pages (which were like newsprint, not glossy, in those days). They always kept the newspapers in the outhouse, which provided reading material and then toilet paper.

Of course, newspapers might clog up the modern plumbing, so if it came to using newspapers, you'd do best to create a private backyard toilet spot where you set up a Porta-Potti so the newspaper can be composted and not sent down the drain.

But what about a situation where it's not practical to have an outdoor toilet?

In the home of Richard White, which doubled as the headquarters for the non-profit organization he founded, he practiced many novel methods of self-reliance, and using less. The sewer line was about two hundred feet down to the main city sewer line, and it was old and always clogging. As a way to avoid clogs until a new sewer line could be afforded, White put a small trash hamper next to the toilet. Into this, he first added a little garden soil and some earthworms. After each toilet use, he would put the toilet paper into the hamper, and close it. He did this for many years. A sign was added so that anyone using the bathroom would know to place their paper into this hamper and not down the drain. On occasion, they used napkins when they ran out of toilet paper, but I don't think newspapers were ever used.

White reported that there was never any smell from this system, probably because of the presence of the earthworm which constantly "ate" and decomposed the toilet paper. Because paper compresses quite a bit, the bin was only emptied every six months or so. When the bin was full, White would take it outside, and put a layer of soil on top of the contents, and wait a few weeks before digging a hole around one of his trees and burying it all. An empty bin was then put back in the bathroom to begin the process all over again.

This method could be employed indoors by anyone who had bad plumbing, or who had to use newspapers and didn't want to flush them down the toilet.

DISHWATER

As already stated, one way to recycle water is to replumb your drain pipes to allow your dishwater to drain into your yard or garden.

If this doesn't seem feasible for you, you can practice a no-cost recycling method: When you're done doing the dishes, take the basin of dishwater outside and manually pour it onto those plants and trees that are the thirstiest. It's so easy to simply carry your dishwater outside and pour it on plants that even if you practice no other form of water recycling, this is one method you should practice.

WASHING MACHINE WATER

Washing machines require quite a bit of water to wash and rinse a load of clothes. The water level on some washing machines can be adjusted to the amount of clothes in the machine, but this is not so with all washing machines.

One way to reduce the burden on your washing machine is to take one or two small items into the bathtub with you each time you bathe, and then hand-wash the items. You'd be surprised what a difference this would make.

I've filled fifty-five-gallon drums with the water from one cycle of a washing machine. After observing how much relatively clean water goes down the drain with every wash, I attempted to find some alternatives.

I've observed that washing machine drain lines are some of the easiest to convert to a grey water system. Washing machines in patios, garages, or outside are the easiest. The closeness of the washing machine to your garden or yard is a factor to consider.

Here are a few possibilities.

At one house where I observed the washing machine water being recycled, the washing machine was located in a service porch. The residents attached a one-and-a-half-inch flexible hose to the drain line and then pushed the hose through a small hole cut into the wood wall, which extended to the outside. Five-gallon buckets were kept outside. When the washing machine drained, someone would go outside and fill the five-gallon buckets, and later take those buckets to the various trees and bushes on the property. Any overflow drained into the soil just beyond the house's outer walkway. This wasn't an ideal system, in my opinion, but it required hardly any outlay of cash, and it was adequate for this household.

I've also seen a flexible hose connected to the washing machine drain line, and the hose was long enough to move around to the various trees and plants on the property. This seemed to be fairly trouble-free. However, in this case, there were three concerns. One, the hose had to pass over a walkway to get to the yard area. Therefore, the end of the hose closest to the washer was kept rolled up outside. When you wanted to use the washer, you attached the hose to the washer's drain line. This took no more than thirty seconds to do. Second, the end of the hose had to be carefully placed since the first water drained often came out hot. Third, the residents had to be careful not to place the outlet of the hose at a lower elevation than the washing machine (the house was on a hill). When they inadvertently did so, siphoning occurred and any new water coming into the washer was siphoned out until the residents observed that this was happening. For this last reason, it's important to thoroughly check out any such system that you develop, and to hire a plumber for assistance if you don't feel able to do so on your own.

I once had a system whereby the washing machine water first went into two fifty-five-gallon drums. The drums were filled with living water hyacinths, which are excellent natural water purifiers. Once the water cooled, I'd open a valve on the lower end of the drums, to which hoses were attached. I'd move the hose to whatever plant or trees I wanted to water.

You need to develop a system to suit your own situation, such as slant of the land, proximity of the washer to the garden or soil, and even such factors as ease of operation. Simplicity of operation is a must. A complicated arrangement may amaze your CalTech buddies, but might turn off your family members who need to use the system day in and out.

Ecological living can and should be practiced especially in the cities. To do so, we must value self-sufficiency as much as—or more than—convenience, and be willing to make a series of minor adjustments in our accustomed wasteful way of doing things.

WASHING CLOTHES
in survival or primitive conditions

Washing machines are another of those devices that modern man seems to think he couldn't live without. Yet for the vast stretch of human history, there were no washing machines. People just washed with hot water and soap and worked the garments by hand until they were clean. Sometimes smooth rocks were used, sometimes not. In fact, sometimes it was just cold running water in the stream and no soap at all.

I once lived in Cuernavaca, Mexico, attending a daily language school. I lived downtown in a tall hotel where many other students stayed, and each day I walked a few miles to my language school, across town up in the hills. To get to school, I walked down and through a canyon on the west edge of town through which a river flowed. This canyon was the poor district, and the people there lived in little square adobe houses, where the window and doors were merely square open-ings in the adobe. A stream flowed through this canyon and every day I'd see how all the people washed their clothes in the stream, usually with rocks. It took me a few minutes to walk through the area where the stream flowed, and I always tried to see what all the people were doing in the river. It was already hot in the morning when I went to school, and the young children were mostly naked, and the women had the clothes stretched out on flat rocks. The clothes had already been soaked in water, and they were rubbing parts of the clothes with small rocks, presumably to take out stains. Later, I was shown the types of rocks used—they were oval shaped, fit into the hand, and though they looked smooth, the surface was actually rough, like fine sand paper. It was a type of decomposed granite, as well as sandstone, that was used. Then they laid the clothes out on the stones to dry in the hot afternoon sun. When I walked home from school, I'd often see them removing the now-dry clothes.

Clearly, a washing machine is not vital to life. But it was invented because people wanted and needed more time to do all the other things in life that they deemed far more important than washing clothes by hand, whatever those other things may be. Clothes are so essential to our daily life—whether in the urban jungle or in the remote outback—that I am often surprised how little attention is given to clothing and fabric selection in the so-called "survival manuals."

TYPES OF FABRICS

Anyone who's ever washed clothes knows that some fabrics clean up better than others, and stains from certain substances are harder to remove than others. In general, from a survival standpoint, I regard cotton and wool (and other natural materials) as superior to any of the man-made synthetic fabrics on the market, with only a few exceptions. Yes, it's true that polyesters will last longer, and will hold up better to rugged abuse, including being washed by stones, but overall, I believe that the comfort and breathability of natural fabrics far outweighs the benefits of synthetics.

Washing in the stream. Photo courtesy Getty Images.

When you're out shopping for clothing in the first place, try to think long term. Will this garment hold up to rugged use? Will I be able to sew it if it tears? Does it have a lot of pockets? Would I be comfortable wearing this if I were suddenly stuck in some disaster and could only wear this for the next two weeks? And read the labels where it tells you how to clean the garment. Those "delicate" garments that should only be taken to a dry cleaner—perhaps you really don't need those garments.

Okay, your clothes are dirty, but you don't have soap or water. Now what? Many times while practicing survival skills in the desert, we'd remove our clothes, shake them out, and lay them in the sun for a bit. Then we'd turn them inside out, and lay them in the sun for another hour or longer. Then, to keep the body clean, my mentor showed us to simply do a dry scrub with a natural bristle brush, which removes dirt and takes off dead skin cells. It may sound like torture, but you really feel refreshed after doing this.

Eventually, you'll get to some water, and you'll want to wash your clothes. Let's begin with soap.

CHOOSING SOAP

A bar of soap is easy to carry. So many people these days are practicing self-reliance skills such as soap-making that you should have no trouble finding a local source of homemade soap. Try local farmers' markets, or try learning the soap-making process yourself. It's really not that hard.

Or, if you don't care for bar soap, just use some liquid detergent and carry it in your pack in a plastic squeeze container. Make sure you twist the lid on tight!

There are endless choices these days in bar soap, or liquid soap, so a lot has to do with your personal preferences. However, if you're going to be camping in the backwoods, do your best to bring along the purest soap you can find so you're not polluting the water, or the soil. Read the ingredients! Avoid coloring agents, and non-natural perfumes.

Here are some of my preferences: When carrying bar soap, I will bring along a bar that was homemade by any of my half-dozen friends who regularly make their own soap. Sometimes I carry Fels Naptha laundry bar soap. For liquid detergent, I sometimes carry Basic H, a completely biodegradable soap. (The only thing wrong with Basic H is the price!) Or, almost as good is Ivory dishwashing liquid. I also like the Seventh Generation soap line.

MAKING YOUR OWN SOAP

MODERN SOAP-MAKING STEP BY STEP

I learned soap-making via a step-by-step class from Kia Bordner, a mother of three daughters who lives in the San Diego area. She began making her own soap when one of her daughters continued to get rashes from commercial soaps.

From start to finish, a batch of soap takes about two hours to mix.

First, get everything together. It would be wise to purchase these supplies and use them exclusively for your soap-making. These include thermometers, kitchen scale, measuring glasses, several containers, wooden spoons, as well as all the oil and lye needed.

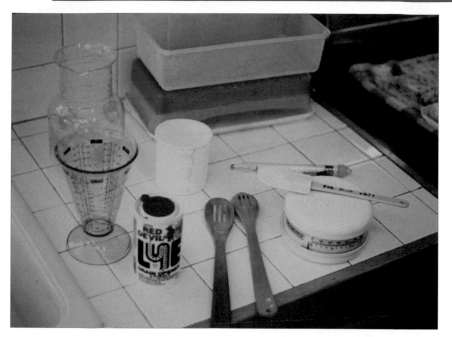

The utensils needed for soap-making. From front clockwise, lye, measuring cup, glass jar for lye, cup, thermometer, spatula, scale, wooden implements. Oil and shortening not shown.

The following is a good beginner recipe for a batch of soap. Once you understand the basics, there are many possible variations.

Everything is measured by weight, not volume.

Measure sixteen ounces of water into your glass container. Add six ounces of lye to the water. Put it in a safe location because it will get hot. Rinse the utensils you just used.

Next, weigh nineteen ounces of vegetable shortening, and put it in a pan to melt. Add twelve ounces of olive oil. After the melting process, the shortening and oil will be about 150°F; turn off the heat once it is melted. You now need to get it down to 98°F.

The lye, which will be hot, also needs to get down to 98°F.

One trick to lower the temperature is to place the container of hot lye and/or hot oil into the kitchen sink. Put some cold water into the sink; this will lower the temperature of the lye and the oil-shortening mix.

Bordner blends the water with the lye. Note that the glass jar is on a mat because it will get very hot.

The lye in this jar is close to 200°F. It must get down to 98°F.

Once both containers—the melted oil and the lye—have reached 98°F, you can pour the lye into the oil, and mix. This is where the saponification occurs. As you mix the oil and the lye, you'll notice how the color changes. Keep mixing, and it may need to be mixed for several minutes. After a while the soap will start to set up, and tracing will occur. (Tracing is where the soap begins to thicken and come off your spoon in a line.)

The soap is poured into a mold.

This is now the stage where you add herbs, flowers, leaves, colors, or other additions of your choice.

For soap molds, you can use plastic boxes that are available at the stationery section of most stores. The container is rubbed with oil or shortening before the soap is poured in so it doesn't stick. Then, the soap is poured into the mold, and the lid is put on.

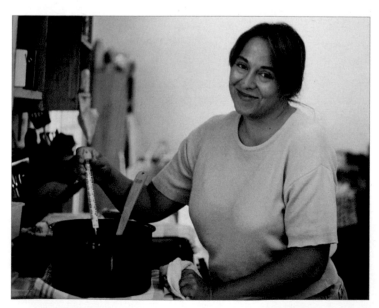

Bordner checks the temperature of the oil. The oil needs to get down to 98°F.

The box is put in a closet, covered with a heavy blanket, and left undisturbed for eighteen to twenty-four hours.

When it is ready to remove, the mold is turned upside down, tapped, and then it falls out. The soap is still not fully hardened, and can be cut into various shapes over the next few days.

That's the condensed version of how to make your own soap. It's a good way to get started. As you get more interested in soap making, you'll find that there are countless recipes for different soaps that are used for different purposes.

Soap-making is a great activity that can involve the whole family. It's educational, and you are not only creating a necessity of daily life, but also an article of barter. Making soap is one of those traditional skills that provides you with a greater degree of self-reliance.

Day-old soap is being removed from the mold.

Soap that has been removed from the mold.

Cutting the soap into useful pieces.

SOAPS FROM NATURE

What if you didn't have the time, or opportunity, to plan? You're just out somewhere, stuck, and among many other things, you need soap. What can you use in nature for soap?

In fact, there are various soap plants found all over North America that have been used for generations by Native Americans and pioneers.

Many (but not all) of the leaves of yucca can be shredded, rubbed with water, and produce a saponin-rich soap. The soap is excellent for washing clothes, sheets, diapers, your hair, your body, your dog, etc.

Fruits and flowers of the widespread Ceanothus genus (mountain lilac) have long been used as soaps, just by rubbing between the hands with water.

In fact, good soap plants can be found throughout North America. You can begin your research into your local soap plants by inquiring at native plant societies, and the botany departments of local colleges.

The leaves of the yucca plant have long been used by Indigenous peoples as a soap. The fresh leaves are shredded and rubbed with water to produce a lather.

The author and students making soap with yucca leaves.

Wild lilac, or Ceanothus, is a wild plant of the Western states whose flowers and sticky fruits were rubbed with water by Indigenous peoples to make a quality soap.

JOJO STONE

Once, while backpacking for a week in the Sequoia National Forest, one of my hiking partners, Jojo, introduced me to another way to stay clean. Each day we took a swim in the river to stay clean, though we had no soap. We'd been handling pine needles to make shelters and we had tar sap and dirt all over our hands and arms. Jojo found a little rock, smaller than a golf ball and oval, whose surface was flat but rough like smooth sand paper. He showed me how to rub my skin with such a rock, and presto!, the pine sap came right off! Ever since, this has been referred to as the "jojo stone."

An example of a "jojo stone."

WASHING BY HAND

I learned to wash my clothes by hand when I didn't have a washing machine. I took one or two small items with me into the bathtub (I took baths, not showers) and hand-washed each item while in the tub. This required approximately fifty to one hundred hard squeezes and some twists and agitations to get the clothing item clean, and then it would be hung out on my "solar clothes dryer." I began to enjoy that process. Soon, I never took trips on my motorcycle anymore with a full load of laundry to a laundromat.

On rainy days, I hung my clothes indoors or in a covered area where they'd dry by the wind, like I saw the Amish do in rural Ohio.

There are a variety of hand-washing devices that can be purchased at Lehman's or Real Goods, or Amazon. For example, consider the scrub board. Personally, I have never cared for this device and never found it useful. But the fact that you see it still being sold must mean that *some* people do find it useful. You can often find these at second-hand stores. You can get one and try yourself and see if you like it.

Timothy Snider shows a scrub board.

There is also a device that I have seen advertised which is essentially a toilet plunger and a five-gallon plastic bucket. This can be easily homemade: You buy a plastic bucket with a lid, and cut a hole in the lid so that you can put the handle of the plunger through the lid. You add your dirty clothes and water and soap into the bucket, and you plunge away! This has its adherents, and it's not that hard to do, though I find that I can get my clothes cleaner just by washing by hand. So a bucket certainly helps when washing clothes in a primitive setting, but I don't find that the plunger is all that essential.

Timothy Snider demonstrates a clothes-washing method using a five-gallon bucket and a plunger.

I have heard various so-called shortcut ways of doing laundry, but most don't really get your clothes clean. These ideas include such things as adding laundry, soap, and water to a plastic bucket, securing the lid, and then rolling it around for awhile. Maybe, but probably not. There's really no substitute for just getting in there and washing your clothes by hand.

NO SOAP?

It may happen that you need to do laundry, but you just don't have any soap. Just washing your clothes by hand in water is better than nothing. Agitate the clothes and just work it until you see the water getting dirty.

For a stain, you can try what I've tried on occasion: I take a small rock, somewhat oval, usually smaller than a golf ball. These are easy to find. Get one with a smooth surface but not too smooth. The surface should feel like fine pumice. Take this rock and gently rub out the stains in your garments. Don't go too hard or you just damage the fibers of the fabric.

Then, while wet, hang the clothes out on a line in the sun, with the stain exposed to the sun.

GETTING OUT STAINS

So you're in the backcountry with minimal supplies, or you're living minimalistically in the city, trying to do as much as you can with

limited income. You still want and need clean clothes. Yes, there are a million stain removers that you can buy at any supermarket, but are there any stain removers that you can make yourself?

Stains can be removed by a variety of methods, depending on what caused the stain, and the type of fabric. And if you don't have those millions of commercial stain removers available, you're going to use one of the tried-and-true methods which have worked forever.

Some of the simple household ingredients used for stain removal.

Your main ingredients to remember for do-it-yourself stain removers will typically include: water, the sun, white vinegar, baking soda, borax, hydrogen peroxide, lemon juice, and alcohol.

SIMPLE STAIN REMOVAL

For a hard-to-remove stain, while the garment is still wet from washing, spray some vinegar water or lemon juice water onto the stain, and place the garment in the sun so the stain is in the sun. The combination of the vinegar water (or lemon juice water) and the sun are often sufficient to bleach out the stain.

HOMEMADE STAIN REMOVER

Mix washing soda (or borax) in equal amounts with white vinegar. Scrub this onto a stain with an old toothbrush and wait ten to twenty minutes before washing.

HOMEMADE SPOT REMOVER

Mix one-and-a-half cups of water, one-quarter cup liquid castile soap, one-quarter cup liquid vegetable glycerin, and put in a spray bottle. Spray the stain as soon as possible, then wash the garment.

STAIN REMOVAL SOAK

Mix one cup of water, one-half cup hydrogen peroxide, and one-half cup baking soak. Soak the stained laundry in this overnight if possible, or pour this mix into your washing bucket with clothes.

INK STAIN REMOVAL

Try using alcohol. If you have an alcohol-based product like a hand sanitizer, try rubbing the stain with that. Try isopropyl alcohol if you have it, and experiment with liquor.

WHERE TO WASH

If you're in the backcountry, don't wash your clothes in the stream. At the very least, think of whomever might be drinking from the stream downstream. If you're using only natural soap from plants you collected, and you're far in the backcountry, perhaps this isn't a big issue. But in general principle, you don't want to pollute the drinking water.

Fill a bucket with water and add your dirty clothes. It's helps to soak the clothes for awhile, if you can, even if just for an hour. Put your bucket in the sun so the water warms up a bit.

If you have a way to heat your water, then heat it on your fire and add the hot water to the bucket. When you're ready to clean, you can go over the garment and scrub particularly bad areas with a brush and soap. In most cases, you can see right away if your scrubbing is getting the stain out. Then, just scrub the garment by hand; I've found that about two hundred hand squeezes are sufficient for the average piece of clothing, and plus you'll be getting a bit of a workout while you're doing this. No need to go to the gym!

If you planned ahead and purchased a solar shower, you can heat your laundry water in the sun and never have to make a fire. (Sometimes a fire is not convenient, and if you're in "enemy territory," it may not be advisable.)

DRYING CLOTHES

Use the power of the sun to dry your clothes! Especially if the power is out, you should get a cord and string up a clothes line.

Julia Russell shows her "old-fashioned" clothes line at her Los Angeles Eco-Home.

BY THE OCEAN

By the way, if you're ever out at sea, or stranded near the ocean, it's a good idea to try and wash your clothes with fresh water as often as possible. Salt, wind, and extreme temperatures of the sea wreak havoc on clothes. Have you ever seen pictures of people who'd been lost at sea for some period of time? Typically, their clothes become rags that just hang on them.

CONCLUSIONS

I found that I had a more intimate connection to my clothes after doing this, and somehow this reminded me of some of Thoreau's commentary, that we should learn to live better with less. I learned what it takes to clean difficult stains, and the different textures of fabrics. I began to buy for sensibility, always buying for wearability and practicality, rarely because something was in style. I would often think before I set out in the morning: What if some disaster befalls me today, and I am forced to wear these same clothes for days or longer? Would my clothes be comfortable? Could I move around easily in them? Could I run? Will they be easy to clean? These and more questions I asked myself, and gradually I eliminated all my clothing that no longer served me.

I consider hand-washing a very normal thing to do. Wash some of your own clothes, hang it up to dry, let the sun refresh it.

Practical survival skills—such as washing your clothes by hand— are not just for the homeless, or squatters, or destitute low-income people, nor are they only for surviving "the end of the world." Survival skills are imminently practical, all the time, everywhere.

CHAPTER SEVEN

INTEGRAL HEALTH

SOME FIRST AID AND NATURAL HEALING CONSIDERATIONS

Living an ecological life necessitates taking as much personal responsibility as possible. This includes taking responsibility for the health of your body....

> *As a retired physician, I can honestly say that unless you are in a serious accident, your best chance of living to a ripe old age is to avoid doctors and hospitals and learn nutrition, herbal medicine, and other forms of natural medicine unless you are fortunate enough to have a naturopathic physician available. Almost all drugs are toxic and are designed only to treat symptoms and not to cure anyone.*
> Dr. Alan Greenberg

"Let your food be your medicine." — Hippocrates

In his book, *The Balanced Diet*, Dr. James Adams stated unequivocally that no drug ever heals; healing is done autonomically by a robustly healthy body ingesting pure foods in a toxin-free environment inside one's home (and vehicles). Much of the teaching of Dr. Adams hearkens back to the wisdom of Hippocrates.

HIPPOCRATIC MEDICINE

Hippocrates' anatomical knowledge was rather scant, but this is compensated for by his profound insights into human physiology and the

soundness of his reasoning. But even so, his surgical techniques for dislo-
cations of the hip and jaw were unsurpassed until the nineteenth century.

In therapeutics, Hippocrates saw the physician as the servant and
facilitator of Nature. All medical treatment was aimed at enabling the
natural resistance of the organism to prevail and overcome the disease,
to bring about recovery.

Hippocrates placed great emphasis on strengthening and building
up the body's inherent resistance to disease. For this, he prescribed
diet, gymnastics, exercise, massage, hydrotherapy, and sea bathing. He
was a great believer in dietary measures in the treatment of disease. He
prescribed a very slender, light diet during the crisis stage of an acute
illness, and a liquid diet during the treatment of fevers and wounds.

Hippocratic medicine was constitutionally based, so its approach
to diagnosis and treatment was quite flexible. As a holistic healing
system, Hippocratic medicine treated the patient, and not just the
disease.

First do no harm

By the way, it is a popular misconception that the phrase "First do no
harm" (<u>Latin</u>: *Primum non nocere*) is a part of the Hippocratic Oath.
Strictly speaking, the phrase does not appear in the oath, though an
equivalent phrase is found in Epidemics, Book I, of the Hippocratic
school: "Practice two things in your dealings with disease: either help
or do not harm the patient." If you want to read the full original
Hippocratic Oath, check it out online or at a library.

HEALING WITH MEDICINAL PLANTS OF THE WEST

Interviewing Dr. James Adams

Health is a foundation factor of "survival." You
can do nothing when you lose your good
health. Food, water, exercise, and more—all
these are the foundations of good health.

And yet, we have a health epidemic
not just in this country, but in the entire

Dr. James Adams.

world. Thousands of people die from complications of surgery, and drugs, every year. The problem, and the solution, is complex; let's deal with just one aspect today.

DR. JAMES ADAMS

Dr. Adams says that the medical profession is mistaken when it comes to how to treat pain. Adams explains that although the brain processes pain, all pain in the body is felt mostly in the organ of skin. However, pain in the mouth and other orifices is felt at the site of the pain, such as a tooth. Therefore, based on his Western medical training, and supported with his Chumash healing training, Adams always treats the skin for all pain conditions. Further, he states that everyone can do such self-medicating "for free," for any pain, with no harmful side effects.

MEDICAL TRAINING

Dr. James Adams is a man on a mission. James Adams teaches pharmacology at USC, and also teaches medical students Chumash healing as part of regular classes. Adams earned his PhD in Pharmacology in 1981 at UC San Francisco in comparative pharmacology and toxicology, and is now an Associate Professor of Pharmacology and Pharmaceutical Sciences at USC. He's written over two hundred articles, both for the lay and academic audience.

Adams got very interested in the medicinal uses of native plants back in 1994. He had been taking his son out on Boy Scout walks and began to realize that all the local plants had been used by the local Native Americans. Adams then set out to find a Native American herbalist to learn from.

He talked with people from the Chumash tribe, but made no progress in finding a skilled herbalist for about two years. Then he heard about Cecilia Garcia and arranged to meet her in the Santa Monica Mountains. Adams brought his wife along, and when he met Garcia, Adams was a bit taken aback by Garcia's request that he sing a song. "I sang a Ponca Indian song," said Adams, "and she told me that it wasn't a very good song, but that I sang it well!"

Then Garcia spent the next two hours talking with Adams' wife, and when it was over, Garcia agreed to work with Adams. "She had to be sure that I wasn't just trying to take advantage of her and exploit her knowledge," explains Adams.

INDIGENOUS TRAINING

Adams then became Garcia's student, and spent fourteen years studying the intricacies, and underlying belief structures, of the Chumash healing traditions.

According to Adams, "I was her apprentice for fourteen years. I worked with her on every aspect of healing, making medicine, gathering medicine, leading hikes, leading talks, leading religious ceremonies, and more. She taught me about the medicine and the Chumash religion. She taught me how to interview patients and reach a diagnosis. She taught me the traditional way to treat patients and how to keep the village productive. We spent many hours and days together, sometimes just the two of us out hiking. We went from Davis to Ensenada and many places in between."

Adams and Garcia eventually collaborated to produce the book *Healing with Medicinal Plants of the West*, which was published in 2005. It's a fully illustrated book which describes the chemistry and uses of the plants that were used by the Chumash for medicine, and generally used throughout the West. Since their collaboration, Adams and Garcia led about one hundred walks and workshops to teach about the native use of healing herbs, until Garcia's untimely death in 2012.

Adams was also instructed by Ted Garcia (chief of the Chumash), his brother Dennis Garcia, their father Ted Garcia, Frank Lemos, and many other Chumash people.

Adams points out that he is accepted by Ted Garcia and the Chumash people who follow him as a healer, but that there are some Chumash people who do not accept him.

Dr. James Adams teaching about the medicinal uses of plants.

OPIOID ADDICTION

I asked Dr. Adams whether or not he was cynical of the medical profession, as I am, or perhaps he believes that doctors are more concerned about making a buck than actually healing a patient.

Neither, he told me. "Doctors are simply working on a false preconceived notion that herbs are not strong enough to deal with certain physical conditions. But believe me, some herbs are just as strong as any patent medicines out there." He adds that there is a lot of good medicine being practiced, but not with the use of opioids for pain.

He points out that there are currently at least 67,000 people who die in the US every year from prescription opioids, and that figure is rising. According to Adams, doctors work from the premise that you should try to control pain by using the drugs that affect the brain. They tell the patient, "let's try x, or y, or z," and when those don't work, they try opioids, like Vicodin.

Adams explained that opioids are compounds synthesized based upon opium's chemistry. This is highly addictive, and has not been shown to work. This is all based on the notion that you need to cure the pain in your brain, but there are no pain receptors in your brain. More than 95 percent of the body's pain receptors are in the skin.

But why have doctors gotten this so wrong, I ask. He tells me that the prevailing theory is still that the brain is the center of all pain, and that pain can be combatted by giving the patient drugs that suppress pain detectors in the brain. "That's the prevailing notion. But the pain comes from the skin," he tells me. The brain might process that pain, but you still need to treat the pain in the skin. "When a child skins their knee, do they quickly grab their brain, or do they grab their knee?" he asks wryly.

It may have been based on the best of intentions, he tells me, but it is not working. "Think of a carpenter who can't do a job with his hammer. What does he do? He gets a bigger hammer. In medicine, pain is often treated with ibuprofen and naproxen. But when that doesn't work, the doctor has a bigger hammer—opioids. And some doctors just go right to that bigger hammer.

A NATURAL SOLUTION

Cecilia Garcia taught Dr. Adams—among other things—the traditional ways to deal with pain. "Cecilia taught me how to make and use liniments from black sage and sagebrush. And as a result of working with several hundred patients over the years, I have seen that these are great pain killers, which also have the ability to deal with chronic pain." Dr. Adams added the science to his corroboration with Garcia, by explaining medically why the Chumash systems work.

"Most modern Western-trained people do not want to believe that the Indian medicines are efficacious," he explains. "I have learned how these herbs worked. It took me a lot longer to learn how they cure chronic pain," adding that he has written several academic papers on this topic.

Two of his papers are "Chronic pain – can it be cured?" in the *Journal of Pharmaceutics and Drug Development 4*, 105, 2017; another is "Control of pain with topical plant medicines" in the *Asian Pacific Journal of Tropical Biomedicine 5*, 93, 2015.

"Everyone says they feel pain in their organs, but it is almost always in the skin. So you put this herb liniment from native herbs on your skin, and the pain is gone. Even kidney stone pain can be treated with the sage brush liniment," he explains.

"We need to learn how to treat pain correctly, and we are not doing that correctly with oral medicines," says Adams. "When I was a boy, everyone knew how to take care of themselves when it came to the most basic everyday medical issues, like using sassafras, yerba santa, and other common herbs. But no one seems to know any of this anymore."

Through his writings and teachings, Dr. Adams hopes to bring back the notion that the body can heal itself if we allow it to do so, and that everyone should take charge of their health, and not assume that the doctor can "heal" us.

BLACK SAGE AND SAGEBRUSH

Adams readily admits that there are some cases that his black sage or sage brush liniment doesn't entirely cure, though there are no side effects either, as in the case of opioids.

He cites an example of a 77-year-old woman with terrible hip arthritis. "She has been making the sagebrush liniment and applying it every day for the last five years, and she says that it keeps her going. Her pain is relieved. And there are dozens of other patients who treat themselves this way, and none have ever reported any incidents of toxicity."

Adams has also been compiling actual testimonials to demonstrate the efficacy of the healing method that he practices.

"Even if a person is told by their doctor that there is nothing the medical profession can do, and that you will die, I say, you are still alive. Your body can heal itself. Don't give up. Learn to live in balance."

Healing with Medicinal Plants of the West is now in its third printing, which includes many of Garcia's recipes for how to use the herbs. Unlike many books on medicinal plants, this one attempts to present the full picture of what it means to be healthy, including the spiritual aspect. There are some prefatory chapters on what's wrong with modern medicine, and how the body must be allowed to heal itself.

Though there is a comprehensive depth to Dr. Adams' scope of teaching, he usually emphasizes that he's not healing anyone, that's he's only making it possible for the body to heal itself. His family came to Virginia from England in 1635, and learned healing from the native Americans to stay alive.

RECIPES [more details are found in Adams' book]

BLACK SAGE SUN TEA: FOOT SOAK FOR ALL BODY PAINS

Dr. James Adams shows the black sage plant.

Soak about one-quarter pound of black sage leaves and stems (Salvia mellifera) in two quarts of water, and set in the sun for several hours until the tea is dark red brown. Strain.

Pour the sun tea into a pan, and soak feet for fifteen to twenty minutes a day for seven days. Refrigerate after each use. Wait one week to see what happens to your pain. Repeat process after second week. This is for any body pains.

One student at one of Dr. Adams' classes soaked his feet in the black sage tea and reported that his chronic neck pain was gone for over a week. "According to James Ruther, "Yes, it worked! I go to the chiropractor every three weeks to manage my condition. My condition is a pinched nerve in my neck. I soaked my feet in the black sage tea and I was pain-free for about a week and a half. My daily pain is more of a discomfort now."

SAGEBRUSH LINIMENT: ELDER'S WINTER MEDICINE

Into a container (he typically uses an eight-ounce Mason jar), place one leaf of white sage. Add four to six pieces of avocado pits (for their oil). Fill the container with as much Sagebrush (Artemisia californica) as you can. Fill the jar with 70 percent isopropyl alcohol. Some use either tequila or vodka instead. Let sit for at least six weeks. Decant, and use the liquid sparingly, as a spray or rub, on those painful parts of the body.

Students soaking their feet in the black sage sun tea.

Soaking feet in the black sage sun tea.

Enrique Villaseñor shows the California sagebrush plant.

Students under the direction of Dr. Adams make the Elder's Winter Medicine.

Dr. James Adams demonstrates how to make the Elder's Winter Medicine.

Students place California sagebrush into glass jars, then add one white sage leaf, avocado seed, and isopropyl alcohol.

For information about Dr. Adams' class schedule, and his several books, contact Adams at www.abeduspress.com.

DR. ADAMS' TESTIMONIAL: YERBA SANTA and ROOT CANAL

On June 17, 2016, I needed to have a root canal. When I was done, dentist gave me a prescription for an antibiotic and a pain killer. Instead, I called Dr. Adams and asked about Chumash herbs that could be used.

His response: Put three yerba santa leaves (Eriodictyon spp.) into a cup and a half of water. Boil that for five minutes. Swish that bitter tea around in your mouth as an antibiotic. There is no need to swallow. Do that morning and evening for four days.

On the first day of using the yerba santa gargle, I swallowed the juice, and thereafter only swished it in the mouth as per the instructions.

During this time, the area of the root canal experienced no pain, and no infection, and no swelling. Nor did any pain or infection develop in the weeks that followed.

The yerba santa plant.

MEET ENRIQUE VILLASEÑOR: AMBASSADOR OF THE PRICKLY PEAR CACTUS

The prickly pear cactus is a super food.

Enrique Villaseñor is at the head of the classroom, extolling the many unsung virtues of the prickly pear cactus. "It's often referred to as poor people's food," he explains, "but did you know that it contains all the essential amino acids, and some non-essential amino acids as well?"

Villaseñor is the defacto ambassador of the humble prickly pear cactus, a plant that has been used for food and medicine for millenia.

After thirty-five years as a school teacher, Villaseñor recently retired and now actively works as an assistant to pharmacologist Dr. James Adams, who shares traditional Chumash healing methods.

In the two-hour presentation, Villaseñor takes his audience through the fascinating history, and the vast healthful benefits, of the prickly pear cactus, beginning with the fact that cacti remnants were found in jars in Mexico dating back 10,000 years. He explains that

Enrique Villaseñor with some ripe prickly pear cactus fruits.

archaeologists have found old jars that contained not only cactus, but teosinte (the forerunner to corn), chili, amaranth, sapote, and mesquite, some of the earliest foods from this continent.

As part of his presentation, Villaseñor shares details from the historical book, *Relación de Cabeza de Vaca,* the account of Álvar Nuñez Cabeza de Vaca's journey in the unknown interior of America. He was one of four survivors of the 1527 Narvaez expedition. From 1527 to 1536, he wandered across the US southwest, learning from the natives about the local foods. Though he was a slave for the first two years, he became both a trader and a healer to the various tribes. He learned of the value of the nopal (aka the prickly pear cactus) from the natives and used it for scurvy, treating arrow wounds, and for stomach issues. After returning to Spain in 1537, he wrote his account of the journey, first published in 1542. Cabeza de Vaca is sometimes considered a proto-anthropologist for his detailed accounts of the many tribes of Native Americans that he encountered.

"The prickly pear cactus is one of the best immune system boosters," says Villaseñor, quoting Hippocrates, who said, "Let food be thy medicine, and let medicine be thy food."

Historically, the prickly pear cactus pads have been used for lowering cholesterol levels, digestive issues, edema, wounds, bronchitis, fevers, vitiligo, inflammation, type II diabetes, muscle pain, urinary problems, burns, and liver problems. Students of Villaseñor listen in

Enrique Villaseñor in front of a large patch of prickly pear cactus.

awe, wondering why they have always considered the prickly pear just a food to eat when you're next to starving, rather than the superfood it is.

Villaseñor explains that because prickly pear was always available in good times and bad, in times of drought and plenty, it was always something that poor people could and did use, but then it came to be regarded as simply a food of last resort.

Today, however, that view is changing. Villaseñor points out that one can find hundreds of products made from the prickly pear on Amazon. This includes food and food supplements, pills for diabetes, as well as various products from the cochineal bug that is often found on the prickly pear plants. The cochineal has historically been dried and crushed to get carminic acid, a very good red dye for clothing and even food products.

The highlight of Villaseñor's presentation is when he turns on a food processor and makes a prickly pear drink for everyone to try.

First, he scrapes the young pads to remove the spines and the tiny hair-like glochids. He puts one large pad into the blender, and adds one apple and one peeled orange, and blends it all. The resultant drink is thick, and can be thinned further with water if one prefers. Everyone enjoyed the tartness and sweetness of the drink. No sugar is ever added.

Before using, each young prickly pear pad must be cleaned of its spines and tiny glochids.

THE RECIPE
Prickly Pear Cactus Smoothie

Note: This recipe is the result of numerous experiments by Villaseñor. This latest refinement of the recipe came about after a visit to Mexico, and seeing the other ingredients added to the drink to make it more flavorful.

Ingredients

1 - Prickly pear cactus pad (cleaned and rinsed)
1 - Peeled orange
1 - Green apple
2 - Kale leaves
2 - Celery stalks
1/3 Bunch of parsley
1/3 Bunch of mint
2 - Cups of chilled water
1 - Cup of ice
1 - Slice of lime

Recipe

Dice one prickly pear pad. The pad should be about average size, with all the spines and tiny glochids cleaned off. Place the pad in a blender with 2 cups of water. Blend. Dice 1 green apple and 1 peeled orange. Blend. Add diced kale, celery, mint, and parsley. Blend. Add additional water to taste if the smoothie is too thick for you. Serve chilled with ice. Use lime to taste. *Do not add sugar.* Suggested serving is 1.5 cups twice a day. Enjoy!

Enrique Villaseñor and Helen Sweany blend the "Agua de Nopales" for students to taste.

According to Villaseñor, this is one of the best ways to get your daily intake of the prickly pear, in a form that is tasty and easy to prepare. The benefits are that it strengthens your immune system, helps you to lose weight, and lowers your cholesterol.

Villaseñor adds that complete health is really about complete balance, and by "balance" he explains that each of us need to find balance physically, spiritually, socially, and financially within our community and family. "You should work at this every day," he explains.

Villaseñor blends all the ingredients for the students to taste.

Blending all the ingredients for the "Agua de Nopales."

Additionally, Villaseñor points out that the natural immune boosters include sleep, plant-based diet, exercise, not smoking, having minimal stress in your life, maintaining a healthy weight, minimal alcohol consumption, maintaining healthy relationships, and avoiding infections. Consuming prickly pear cactus daily is just one part of this overall balance.

Villaseñor shares a little about his background during his presentation. His mother is still alive at 101 years old, and she taught him balance in all things. "I was outside all day, always doing things outdoors," he explains. "And when we had a problem, my mother healed us!"

Villaseñor also shares testimonials from students of his and Dr. Adams, students who have experienced lower glucose levels, improved bowel movements, weight loss, and lower cholesterol levels by consuming the prickly pear cactus drink, and other herbal remedies they teach.

Regarding the many additives to foods today, Villaseñor advises, "If you cannot pronounce it, do not eat it!"

Villaseñor smiles as he shares an old idiom, which underscores how Mexico's identity is tied to the nopal, or prickly pear cactus. "Soy

Villaseñor conduct a traditional blessing with a sage leaf at the beginning of each of his classes.

más Mexicano que el nopal," he says, which translates as, "I am more Mexican than the cactus." The expression is asking, between the lines, what came first, the Mexican or the cactus, affirming the person's pride in being Mexican.

Enrique Villaseñor can be contacted at <u>Senornopales@gmail.com</u>.

HOT WATER THERAPY

When I first met Richard White and became his student, he introduced his students to many disciplines and regimens for the improvement of the body and of the mind.

One of these methods was a hot water therapy that anyone could practice in their own bathtub. When he taught his students this regimen, White always pointed out that the skin is the largest organ of the human body, and as an organ of excretion, it was of paramount importance to keep the pores "open and breathing."

Here is a brief overview of the method, but keep in mind that when White taught this, there were many more nuances and fine details than I'd have space for here. Here are the main points of instruction for what he called "entubification." He emphasized that this is about the "science of atonement," and that one should do this with the same precision as a science experiment.

Into an empty tub, add the hottest water, just enough to cover the bottom. Let it stand for about ten minutes and then drain. Then let the hottest water slowly drip back in. The dripping sound is therapeutic to the nerves. It also helps to keep the water at a constant temperature, and tends to block out other noises that might be distracting. (White's method did not involve filling a tub and getting in. Furthermore, his bathtub drain was disconnected from the sewer line so that all the draining water went into his orchard.) Add skin conditioners and top-quality soap. Originally, White recommended Basic H, a top-quality product, but in time he switched to other soaps. ("The only thing wrong with Basic H is the price," he would tell us.) He also added lemon peels, jade leaves, a little olive oil, and eventually other ingredients.

Hopefully, the bathroom has the possibility of cross-ventilation for the replenishment of oxygen. He suggested leaving the door open about one-and-a-half inch for every person in the room. (Often White was alone when he did this procedure, and we would note that he kept a baseball bat near his tub, "just in case.")

Add an article of personal clothing into the tub, under the drip, and let it soak. White always said that it was best to wash such items that touch the skin, like a t-shirt. Also, always watch to make sure there are a few suds there; if there are none, add a little more soap.

Lay in the tub on your back, with your feet elevated.

Force your spine down onto the tub, especially the lumbar ("back hump") and the cervical (neck) while there is hot water surrounding. "This is meant to be work," said White. You hold down the spine as long as you can, to your limit. Then, you relax, and between the pushings, you concentrate your attention wholly on the sound of your breathing. Your eyes are focused on the bridge of your nose. (Remember, White was also a Yoga instructor and this bears a resemblance to certain Yoga asanas.) Then begin to press the spine again, to your limit. Then focus on the breathing again. This cycle is repeated at least three times, while keeping the water temperature between 100° and 105°F.

By now, the body should be in a state of mild perspiration. Wash with your body soap again. Get a full lather in your hair and leave it there.

Practice "thinking without creating thoughts." This was a key aspect of White's other teachings, and it is based on the writings of Harold Percival's *Thinking and Destiny*.

By now, the tub should be about two-thirds full. With your hands, hard squeeze your clothing item at least one hundred times, while breathing deeply in and out. For various reasons, White always said, "Do not ring the clothing. Hard hand squeezes only."

Next, turn off the dripping water, and scrub the entire body once. This scrubbing often took White a very long time, as he literally worked over every square inch of his body. He would use a boar bristle brush, and sometimes a plastic Fuller brush. Everyone has to find the brush that's right for their skin. When done, the body is submerged and rinsed, and the water is allowed to drain out (hopefully into the garden).

Once the tub is drained, then the plug is put back in and the tub is filled to about two inches of hot water. While that's happening, you do some more squeezing of your clothing item. You turn off the water, do a final lather with the body soap, rinse, and then again drain the water.

Then, you rinse again with hot water, and finally, hold your head under the faucet and rinse the head with cold water and massage briskly with your fingers.

Because one's body was experiencing high temperatures while doing this, and thus under stress, White also suggested that the purest water, or fruit juice, be sipped all during the time in the tub.

The whole procedure could take anywhere from thirty to sixty minutes, though White often spent a few hours in the tub! He recommended this procedure at least every three days. He eventually produced a lengthy list of all the sicknesses and illnesses and skin conditions that he believed were cured with this technique, such as colds, flus, upper respiratory problems, eczema, and many others.

THE MEDICINE FINALLY WORKED...
Some experiences with the remarkable ALOE VERA plant

Sometime in late 1978, my mother shared with me one of her experiences with the aloe vera plant. My mother, Marie, was a registered nurse who worked at a Pasadena retirement home as the staff nurse. About three months earlier, a housekeeper who lived on site at the retirement home began to break out in a hive-like rash that caused her to itch constantly. The cause was said to be a nervous condition. The patient's thighs, back, arms, shoulders, and neck all broke out in this rash, which the patient described as "burning like fire."

My mother offered to apply the juice of the aloe leaf to the patient's red spots, but the patient responded, "No, I'll have the doctor check it." The doctor came and prescribed Atarax (internally) for the itching and allergies, and cortisone (externally), which was applied as a cream. The doctor also prescribed tranquilizers for sleep.

After about forty-five days, the patient, Lucille, told my mother that she still could not sleep at night, and that the rash hadn't improved. Lucille noted that there was a slight improvement in the rash when she stayed home and didn't go to work, so Lucille and the doctor assumed this was a nervous condition associated with work.

So my mother, Lucille's nurse, asked again if she'd like to try some aloe. Lucille responded, "Yes, please, bring me anything!" Lucille was a bit frantic, since she'd barely slept in forty-five days and the rash hadn't improved, despite the doctor's prescriptions. My mother noted that Lucille's skin was hot to the touch, and there were big red spots all over.

At 7:30 a.m., my mother took a fresh succulent aloe vera leaf, slit it open, and rubbed the gel onto Lucille's arms, legs, back, neck—almost her entire body. Lucille said her skin *immediately* felt better. By 3:30 p.m. that afternoon, all the red spots were gone, and Lucille happily told my mother that all of the burning itching was gone. The next day, Lucille told my mother that the previous night was the first night she'd slept in a long time.

My mother had been somewhat reticent to apply the aloe because she was subservient to the doctor, and could have lost her license by doing something "medical" without the approval of the doctor.

When the doctor arrived, Marie told him that Lucille's rash had cleared up, and she admitted to having applied aloe juice. The doctor was somewhat taciturn as he examined the patient, and, without commenting on the aloe, told my mother, "It's good that the medicine finally worked." Really?!

My mother always had a laugh re-telling this story about a doctor who couldn't see the obvious. Eventually, the other nurses referred to my mother as the "witch-doctor" because she used aloe and various other natural methods of healing, behind the doctor's back.

Over the years, I had my mother document the many cases where she used aloe to cure various skin conditions, on her patients, herself,

A mature aloe vera plant.

even the cats. She also used aloe for sunburn, burns from hot oil, skin sores, diaper rash, bed sores, and poison oak rash.

In one case, our family cat had a large open ulcer on his thigh; we weren't sure of the cause, but we presumed that the cat had gotten into a fight. My mother directed me to put some of fresh aloe gel onto the ulcer every day for three days, while also making some of the aloe leaf into a juice, which was added to the cat's water. The wound was completely healed after three days. "It was unbelievable," expressed Marie, "but it worked!"

My mother's experiences took place over forty years ago, and today aloe vera is a common household word. You can buy it anywhere, even Trader Joe's markets. And as the succulent plant was studied and researched all these years, many have come to call it a miracle herb.

The properties of aloe are a broad mix of antibiotic, astringent, pain inhibitor, emollient, moisturizer, antipruritic (reduces itching), as well as a nutrient. It apparently works because of the polysaccharides present, the main one of which is a glucomannan. Other ingredients of the aloe include galactose, uronic acids, and pentoses. The miracle qualities of the aloe are not believed to be the polysaccharides alone, but the synergistic effect of these and other compounds in the leaf.

Many have tried to create an aloe product that you can buy in a bottle, and some are quite good. I've had some good results from the aloe drink that I have purchased at Trader Joe's market. But please make no mistake about it: the best results come from the gel from the freshly broken leaf of aloe. And though aloe vera seems to be the best, any of the juice from any aloe can be used for burns, poison oak, and so on.

Every homestead—especially urban homesteads—should have plenty of aloe growing, so the fresh leaf is always handy to use when needed.

VINEGAR OF FOUR THIEVES

We're very advanced here in the US, and there's no reason we should ever be concerned about anything as drastic as bubonic plagues, right? Oh, so wrong! Plague is spread by fleas on the rats, which are common when the level of general hygiene drops. Though we haven't seen anything like this (yet) in the US—not even the most recent COVID-19 death numbers came close to some of the historical plagues—let's look at how four thieves managed to deal with plague conditions.

During an outbreak of bubonic plague in France several centuries ago, four thieves managed to loot empty plague-ridden homes without contracting the dreaded plague. After all, they figured, what did it matter? Nearly everyone was dead. Some Middle Ages accounts tell us that during some of the worst plague outbreaks, the dead outnumbered the living, and the dead could not be buried fast enough.

These four thieves were arrested by the police for looting, and were brought before the French judge in Marseilles. Wondering aloud, the judge asked how it was that these four thieves managed to resist the plague, especially since they had been in and out of so many plague-infested homes.

"We drink and wash with this vinegar preparation every few hours," they answered. The judge made a shrewd bargain. The thieves would be given their freedom in exchange for their "anti-plague recipe."

This recipe is recorded in Dian Buchman's *Herbal Medicine* book. Buchman writes, "This recipe has been used for centuries, but legend has it that it was discovered during a devastating bubonic plague."

Here's the recipe:

Vinegar of Four Thieves
2 quarts (half gallon) apple cider vinegar
2 T lavendar
2 T rosemary
2 T sage
2 T wormwood
2 T rue
2 T mint

Combine the herbs and steep in vinegar in the sun for two weeks. Strain. Add 2 T of garlic buds and steep for several days. Remove. To preserve, add 4 oz of glycerin.

Karin James, the editor of the *Forest Voice*, adds that the vinegar recipe can be used for washing floors, walls, and windows, and will offset smells in the home. It helps to deter bugs if you rinse your hiking gear in it. She also saves the herbs when she strains them out of the vinegar, and places them where ants come into the kitchen. "It works," she states. "No more ants!"

We posted this recipe on our website and got many responses from readers. One suggested that it is the vinegar which is the primary reason why this recipe worked. We have used raw apple cider vinegar (in our drinking water, in a ratio of about two teaspoons per quart) and have found that it keeps the mosquitoes from biting us, and helps reduce heat stress when working out in the sun. Whole books have been written about the health benefits of vinegar. We strongly suggest you always use only the raw apple cider vinegar.

While we certainly hope that we're never going to have to worry about outbreaks of bubonic plague, health authorities point out that the plague has never entirely disappeared. In fact, it is still found in the

Garlic

Daniella shows some garlic cloves and raw apple cider vinegar, two ingredients in the "Vinegar of Four Thieves."

fleas of squirrels living in the nearby mountains. Conditions of poor hygiene are the breeding grounds for rats and plague.

Ubiquitous homeless camps, with no running water, toilets, or hygiene conditions, provide a conducive condition for plague to spread again. While we certainly hope that efforts to assist homeless are more and more successful, it's nevertheless valuable to look to the past for one solution to this problem.

References:

The Balanced Diet, Dr. James Adams

Vermont Folk Medicine, D.C. Jarvis, MD

Prickly Pear Cactus Medicine: Treatments for Diabetes, Cholesterol, and the Immune System, Ran Knishinsky

Illustrated Encyclopedia of Natural Remedies, C. Norman Shealey, MD

CHAPTER EIGHT

UTILITIES: LIVING BETTER WITH LESS

If you choose to live a low-impact, ecological, and economical lifestyle, you're going to be taking a closer look at all of the "automatic" uses of utilities (gas, electric, water) that we've simply been taking for granted. Consider the idea that you can actually live well, and maybe even better, by choosing to use *less* than you are currently losing. You are not "losing" by choosing to use less; rather, you are gaining in the quality of life, and possibly even in the amount of time you have for what you might consider the "important things" in life. Let's look at many of our popular uses.

ELECTRICITY

There are so many tasks that we do automatically in today's world with electricity. Let's explore the many ways you could perform these tasks without electricity. Maybe you just want to be independent. Maybe you want to save money. Maybe you want to live remotely and having an electrical line is impractical, or too expensive. Whatever the reason, let's take a look at how would you handle "normal" tasks if there were no power.

REFRIGERATION

We take electricity for granted when it comes to food refrigeration. After all, the average person living today doesn't have to worry about food spoiling quickly, as people did in the pre-electric days. But if the power went out for extended periods of time, you should eat the most perishable food in your refrigerator first. After that, think about the traditional ways of storing food, since that's what you'll be doing to store food. Any food must be dried, or canned, or pickled, or in the coolest parts of your home, such as the cellar or cooler.

We also keep some of the "blue ice" packs in the freezer. In the event of an outage, they might effectively extend the cooking time of whatever we have in the refrigerator.

LIGHTING

These are some emergency photo-voltaic systems which are designed strictly for lighting. Other possibilities include the old standards: candles, oil lamps, and flashlights. Purchase as many candles as possible from the hardware store (don't waste your money on ornamental candles—just buy the simple utility candles). Lights: oil lamps, candles, flashlights, solar lamps.

Dude McLean shows his Dietz lantern for camping and emergencies.

Oil lamps can be purchased at department stores, hardware stores, some supermarkets, and even yard sales. Most are quite simple. Just make sure you know what sort of fuel your lamp burns, and stock up. You may also need to buy a few extra wicks.

If you want a top-quality emergency (or remote cabin) lantern, we recommend any of the lamps sold by companies such as Aladdin, Coleman, and others manufactured for the backpacking and camping industry.

Do you already have plenty of flashlights? We have flashlights throughout the house, and several are mounted in different rooms for easy access. Buy and store batteries also. We have several battery chargers that are powered by the sun. This means you are self-reliant with batteries, since—if you follow the recharging instructions—you can get up to ten years of use from some of the modern rechargeable batteries.

You must make certain, however, that you are buying the right recharger for your batteries. In some cases, it will not matter which batteries go into which recharger, so you need to ask and find out. Generally, for home use, you will be purchasing either nickel-cadmium rechargeable batteries, or the new generation alkaline batteries.

TELEVISION

Yes, we can all survive without television. It is not essential to our health or well-being. After the Northridge, California, earthquake, we had no electricity for a day or so, and there was no threat to our life, health, or well-being. We realized, though, that we were very curious about what was going on in the outside world. How bad was the damage? What was being done? Was there anything we could do?

The radio was somewhat useful in getting information. Our phone line was out. In the week after the quake, we went to Target in Pasadena and purchased a small battery-operated television for about $50.

RADIO

Again, battery-operated radios, though not critical to your life and health, can keep you informed if the power goes out due to earthquakes, or whatever.

We are very impressed with the various hand-crank radios now available. You crank a dial for one minute and you can listen to the radio for about thirty minutes. They are not just junky toys, but appear to be quality products which definitely have their place.

If you cannot locate one, please contact us and we'll let you know where you can purchase one. There are several companies which now

One example of the hand-crank radios available. This one also has a solar panel.

manufacture these ingenious crank radios, some of which also have a solar panel so they can simply be placed in the sun to get power.

BACK-UP BATTERY

If you rely upon your computer for your work, communication, or education, you should investigate a back-up battery pack, and a simple photo-voltaic system designed to provide at least the minimal amount of electricity needed to keep that computer running.

There are manual counterparts for many of the tasks or tools for which we commonly rely upon electricity. Here are some common-sense alternatives to electricity that you could employ by choice, or in the event of a blackout, when you had no choice.

WASHING MACHINE

No power, no washing machine, right? True, but did folks ever wash their clothes in the pre-electric days? Of course they did. They used a combination of the following: hot water, their hands, soap. Yes, folks, you can wash your clothes by hand, rinse them, and hang them out to dry.

CLOTHES DRYER

A modern clothes dryer is fantastic for certain articles of clothing. However, if you don't have one, or don't want one, there is always the ancient stand-by: the solar clothes dryer. I always prefer the low-tech solar clothes dryer, available for the cost of the cord at your local hardware store.

VACUUM

Electric vacuums have their place, but if you're choosing to only use for essential needs, use a mop, use a broom, and shake out the rugs.

ELECTRIC CAN OPENER

I am surprised how often I have been at someone's home and they could not open a can because either the electric can opener was broken or the power was out. Our addiction to convenience has created a nation of electricity addicts, where we believe we cannot function without it. Go to the hardware store or supermarket and buy a manual can opener. In a pinch, I have opened cans with the can opener blade of my Swiss Army knife.

A manual can opener, juicer, and grater—all operated by hand.

MICROWAVE OVEN

Get rid of it! Yes, I know, it can be argued that they don't really use that much electricity, and obviously they cook fast, but you might be amazed how the quality of your life, and your relationship to your meals, will improve when you go back to simple cooking of your meals.

FOOD BLENDER

As a child, I recall making whipped cream with a fork. Yes, it took a long time, but we had the time since no one was paging us and we had no e-mail to check. Nearly all "food processing" can be done with an assortment of knives, spoons, forks, and a few other assorted items normally found in any kitchen.

COFFEE GRINDER

When we started looking for hand-crank coffee grinders, we were dismayed at the low quality of products on the market. We began looking for coffee grinders at yard sales and flea markets, and over the years have purchased over a dozen old-fashioned, well-made coffee grinders. These are the type with the wooden box that you sit on a table or in your lap, with the hopper on top and a large handle. We have typically paid from $10 to $25 for these. Not only are they functional and better than any of the modern grinders on the market today, but they are also attractive conversation pieces.

HEATING AND COOLING

We are so hooked on electricity that our entire society operates with the notion that cheap electricity will always be available. This includes the way we build homes, with no concern about orientation to the sun, and no concern about natural air flows and currents. We end up with an energy-inefficient home with its constant high costs of operation.

AUTOMATIC DISH WASHER

Get rid of them! You might get some money for them from a scrap metal yard.

GARBAGE DISPOSALS

Get rid of them! There are many reasons why garbage disposals are not a good choice. For one, you are always inviting plumbing problems. Plus, does it really make sense to "grind up" all your so-called "garbage" and flush it down the drain? We don't think so. Even if you live in an apartment, a compost pit somewhere outside can be made.

We never discard food wastes or "garbage." If we cannot feed it to Otis (our pot-bellied pig), or our dogs, or the chickens, or other animals, then we "feed" it to our combination worm farm/compost pit.

"Waste disposal" is a serious problem for all urban areas, and especially after any sort of breakdown of normal public services. We strongly suggest you learn how to do as much of your own waste disposal as possible, and make it a part of your everyday life. If you have specific questions about this, feel free to contact us.

ELECTRIC CLOCK

We have a few, of course, but we also have battery-operated clocks and wind-up clocks. Time-keeping can be critical at all times, but even more so in the aftermath of a major urban disaster where you will need to meet others at set times, or for other times where strict coordination of schedules is required. We strongly urge you to have at least one wind-up clock in the house.

HEATING WATER

Heating the water in your home would be more difficult without the convenience of gas heaters. Since we'd be primarily interested in hot water for bathing, you'd have to simply heat the water, pot by pot, on a woodstove or backyard fire.

We have purchased a Magamex water heater, made in Mexico, which heats the water through the use of a small wood fire underneath. Obviously, such a heater must be placed in a safe location, but as long as you have water under pressure, you have hot water where you need it. *[Note: As of about 2010, the Magamex company is no longer in business, though there are other companies which manufacture similar wood-fired water heaters.]*

Years ago I visited a remote mountain cabin in the Angeles National Forest. The stone cabin was square, perhaps twenty feet by twenty feet. In the very middle was a large cinderblock stove and fireplace. One side opened into the living room, which was one entire half of the cabin. It had been designed so that a small vent went from the fireplace into the bedroom for heating. The kitchen comprised the other quarter of the interior space, and I never forgot the unique stove. It was large, designed for wood, and just off to one side sat a water tank with about a fifteen-gallon capacity. From the bottom of the tank, galvanized pipes led the water into the stove's firepit to heat the water. Of course, hot water rises. This tank was plumbed to the sink, located just to the left, so that when you turned on the hot water, you forced the water through the pipes (where they were heated, if you had a fire), into the tank, and then out the spigot. This was just one example of a well-designed mountain cabin that took nature's forces into account.

CHAPTER NINE

ALTERNATE COMMUNICATIONS

This is an introduction to the alternate forms of communication that would be available if our land-based telephones go out due to a computer glitch, an earthquake, a hurricane, a terrorist bomb, etc. Remember that ANY alternative system still requires electricity from some source, whether it is a photo-voltaic electric panel or batteries. Vehicle-mounted radios are okay, as long as you have gas to run the vehicle, and as long as you keep in mind that you are wearing down the battery when you run the radio if the car is not running.

For my basic research, I spoke with Dave Strom, author of Power Up, which is about battery adapters for military radios. Strom emphasized that whatever alternative system you eventually go with, the quality of your antennae is the most critical factor since that is what will be receiving and transmitting.

Communications fail in most emergencies. It's a sad but simple fact of life. Most folks have had the experience of seeing an accident on the freeway and then the cell service over loads, or is spotty at best. This happens to landline service as well as the internet. Like our freeways, the system can handle a limited amount of traffic.

Many folks today think that most of the world's communication is wireless or via satellite. However, the reality is that most communication is handled by landlines. Cell sites are connected to various landline services. "Submarine cables" on the bottom of the ocean connect continents.

Readers should understand that I have no financial interest in any of the companies I mention. I wish I did.

CELL PHONE

Here are a few recommendations on cell service. They will apply to the new "5G" as well. Text messages can get through during "normal" busy times. However, these typically fail in extended or widespread emergencies.

You will need charging cables, cigarette lighter adapters, etc., to fit your equipment. These are cheap but easily lost or damaged. Spares should be kept in each car as well as in your bug-out pack, EDC, etc. Phone cover/carry case. These can really save the day if you drop the phone. Waterproof bags for your gear, simple zip-lock bags may do the job.

Battery "power banks" are a great idea. They are about the size of a cell phone but are simply a battery pack that you pre-charge and then use to recharge/power you phone.

When your internet is down, you need to receive information. Your monitoring station capability starts with something you already own. Often over looked, the AM/FM radio in your car or other AM/FM radio.

In fact, the simple AM radio will become one of the most important intelligence-gathering tools you can have. If you are caught unprepared, this simple radio will be extremely important.

Obviously, you can tune in the local stations in your area. However, in widespread disasters, these may not be working. The next step will be to tune slowly across the AM band at night. These frequencies can travel hundreds of miles at night. It may or may not be as clear as you are used to. However, you will likely find stations you can understand.

In southern California, on the way to work at 5 a.m., I used to listen to stations from Arizona, Utah, and many others on the AM dial in

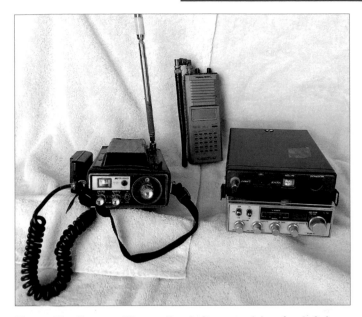

These old radios are still operational after several decades. Left, is a Midland CB from the '70s. The built-in antenna and battery pack have allowed five mike contacts. Center: a 30-year-old scanner. Right, a Mobil CB with SSB, allowing greater range. Normally mounted in a truck, this one's attached to an old Radio Shack Portable Power Pack. This allowed use on the move or at remote locations.

my truck. Some will be "Clear Channel Stations." These are intended to stay on in emergencies, usually have emergency power, and are high-power stations. Stations in other areas will shut down allowing the frequency or "channel" to be "clear" to reach long distances.

If you have an old-school analog radio, it is simply a matter of tuning slowly across the band. When you find a station, you'll need to pause and listen. Headphones can be a big help. Note the time, frequency, and station call sign and location for reference. This is your station log. You may need to return to this station.

If your radio is digital, the scan function will likely only lock on to local stations. Use the "tune" button to work across the band. Take your time and wait a few seconds after each time you push the tune button. This will seem tedious but in troubled times, the announcer will be reading unfamiliar terms, and may pause often.

Using a portable radio, you may need to turn the radio itself to the right or left. The AM antenna is inside the radio.

Years ago, finding these distant (DX) stations was a hobby. You can practice this tonight with the radio in your car. Or follow the above instruction on your way to work. You'll learn a useful skill during your commute.

SHORT-WAVE RECEIVER

The next step in the monitoring is having a so-called "short-wave receiver." Many countries have stations that intentionally broadcast to the world. Well-known are: England's BBC World Service as well as Radio Moscow, Radio France, etc. The dials of old radios often had the country's name on the dial for easy location.

There are many of these radios, but I find the KATO brand easy to use, rugged, and reasonable priced. The TECSUN radio is a very good small radio. Many thanks to my cousin and close friend, Jerry, for sending me this rig. There are many other brands and prices. These receivers can also tune in the ham radio HF bands. This alone may give you a wealth of information.

SCANNER

Last in the monitoring station area are scanners. These can be base stations, mobile, or hand-held. Be sure to check your area's regulation for mobile use. In some areas, you cannot have one in a car unless you are a licensed ham radio operator.

A scanner, after programming, switches automatically through frequencies. When it hears a transmission, it stops so you can hear the message. It does this rapidly so you hopefully won't miss anything. Typically, they are used to monitor police and fire department's communications.

"Trunked" radio systems are used by most police and fire departments and other city agencies. However, many are using "digital trunked systems." So you will need to be sure your scanner will allow you to do this. There are many on the market for your selection.

If you only have an older scanner or are using a ham radio for this reception, you can still find a tremendous amount of radio traffic.

Tow trucks, school buses and related maintenance crews, utility companies, etc., all can provide information for you.

TWO-WAY COMMUNICATIONS

Communicating with your family and friends will be extremely important in emergencies. This might be while driving, patrolling, or foraging.

Your best option is to become a licensed amateur (ham) radio operator. With your license, you have local and worldwide communications. High Frequency, called HF, gives you worldwide communications. VHF and UHF allow local contacts. Using ham satellites, you can talk to the world from a hand-held radio.

In cities or rough terrain, a repeater is typically used. You might be on one side of a mountain and your friend on the other. Since you can't talk to one another, a repeater is used. This type of radio receives your signal and retransmits immediately to another frequency that your friend receives on. These things happen in a split second and you are talking in "real time."

There is a test to qualify, but anyone can pass with some study. Joining a local ham club will help you greatly. Many clubs own repeaters you can use, and this is a great value to you. Contact the ARRL for more information and club listings. Ham operators are great folks and you will find a wealth of knowledge and help.

Shown are three modern hand-held ham radios. On the left is a Chinese import, inexpensive and feature-packed.

Center, a real work horse radio, the Yeasu 411 is about 25+ years old, and works like new. Right, the Yeasu VX5R, small and very rugged.

With a ham license, you will only be talking to other licensed hams. This means your family and friends will need to test also. If your spouse, family, or friends are not interested in ham radio, you still have options. In these cases, I strongly recommend at least one person per family become a ham. The knowledge you gain will help you in the other radio services you might use such as GMRS.

GENERAL MOBILE RADIO SERVICE

GMRS is "The General Mobile Radio Service." These are UHF radios which can be home based, mobile, and hand-held. There are repeaters to extend your range as described above. You pay for the license and it covers your family.

To use the repeaters, you typically join an organization that is similar to a club. You will likely be using commercial radio equipment. Many times, the easiest way to get into this is to contact local commercial radio suppliers. They are often a great source of information and you can get going ASAP. Also, check the FCC and the "Personal Radio Steering Group."

FRS is the Family Radio Service. These are small UHF radios and are often seen in discount stores in "blister packs." They share several of the GMRS frequencies. They are very low power and cannot legally use external antennas.

FRS radios are unlicensed but very useful to have and inexpensive. You can buy several and hand them out to other drivers in a small convoy, on a hike, use for youth groups, etc. What's not to love about that! No repeaters are involved.

Other "blister pack" radios that are using GMRS frequencies are higher powered and likely require licensing. These often change in cosmetics and model names. So, you MUST read all the "fine print" to verify requirement in licensing.

OTHER

If you own a boat, you might use the marine radio service. There are VHF and long-distance HF channels. Start with the US Coast Guard at navcen.uscg.gov.

MURS is the Multi User Radio Service. No license is needed and the radios are simple to use. I find MURS to be rather under-used. You can have limited outside antennas, but are very useful.

CB

Lastly, there is CB radio. It retains some of the stigma from the craze in the 1970s. CB radios are a tool, and used as intended, are a fine radio for the right job. These are unlicensed so anyone can use them. While not commercial nor military quality, they are more rugged than you might think. Monitoring the truckers can still be a useful information source for you. Many today have the US weather channels and SSB capability. The latter often has more "reach" that the AM mode.

CB had many "problem" operators, but most have faded away.

You can use external antennas on the home or in the car. At times you can get about 5 to 30 miles range from these. Hand-held versions often have connections for external antennas, power, etc. I once helped a Scout group add external antennas, power, and miscellaneous to their old Radio Shack hand-held CB radios. They had clear, reliable communications two miles up a canyon's winding road.

In the 1970s, we used CBs for finding gas during the shortages. Also, at times in California, there were "smog checks." These were something like the "sobriety checkpoints" seen today. Driving hot rods, we were big targets for these. CBs were used to avoid those places.

SOURCES

Power for your emergency radio gear is as close as your local Harbor Freight. Their small solar systems are a good start for many people. Add their portable power pack at around $50 and you have a nice start.

Your new friends at the ham radio club can guide you through this. Obviously, I am strongly recommending you join an active ham radio club.

For further information on ham radio start with the Amateur Radio Relay League (ARRL), which is the organization for ham operators Network. Also check with the American Redoubt Radio Operators Network (AMRRON), which encompasses various radio services including ham, CB, etc.

Books on CB radio are available. I recommend two books. The first is *The Screwdriver Experts Guide to CB Radio Repair,* a great book and much is applicable to other antenna systems, proper installation, testing, etc. The other book is *Understanding and Repairing CB Radios,* also very good, with a section on homemade test gear which alone is worth the price of the book. Both are written by Lou Franklin, and published by CB City International.

This should give you an outline of how to start your "off grid" communications systems.

FIRST-STEP ADVICE FROM DAVE STROM

"In a group or family, I would strongly suggest that one person do the work to get a ham license and become the specialist. Communication is a specialized art. Then, that person will begin to see all the other things they can do. At least one person should have this technical knowledge of communication so that, among other things, if a component fails, that person will know how to get the system up and running again.

"All communication gear should have the option of charging from a car, that is, from 12 volts.

"I would choose models that can use an external antenna. With this capability, you can connect your radios to antennas that are mounted on a car or to antennas that effectively increase your power. Many antennas can be homemade from recycled materials."

CHAPTER TEN

BETTER USE OF RESOURCES

The person who is trying to live minimally, buying very little and using only what is needed, is choosing to live in a manner that anyone living in a time of war, famine, or scarcity would be required to live.

If the world you know explodes with war, famine, economic collapse, tidal waves, a comet hitting the earth, nuclear radiation, terrorist attacks, something, then you're not likely to have functioning stores with full shelves.

A minimalist providing for his or her basic needs goes through the mental process that the survivor of war goes through: How do you provide for your most basic day-to-day needs?

These needs never change. You need water, food, shelter, and clothing. Beyond those very basic things, you need tools to make things. You need the tools to make the tools to grow and process food, to make new shelters (temporary or otherwise), to make clothing and footwear. If you have the know-how, you might be able to utilize electrical devices, and maintain bicycles for transportation.

In the aftermath of a major calamity, there's no telling what you might find in the piles of rubble. In the case of someone choosing to live as a minimalist, you can choose to do with less, and you can choose to re-use resources many times to fulfill your needs.

If you're a creative recycler, you already know that there are many things you can do with discarded items. And if you grew up poor, you probably already know that you can take the most far-flung objects and figure out how to use them to serve whatever your needs happen to be.

So let's look at the types of trash that are common, and the needs that these might fulfill.

Keep in mind that although we all have the same basic needs, those needs vary depending on the season, our age, gender, state of health, and perhaps most important, the skills we possess and the network of friends that we maintain.

With a well-balanced variety of survival and self-reliance skills, you should be able to use a broad variety of raw materials to fix things, make things, and grow food. With a broad social network, you should have someone who can do just about anything, and you have the ability to trade.

THINGS WE MIGHT FIND IN ABUNDANCE

Just like there are the four food groups (meat, dairy, grains, fruits/vegetables), there are the four trash groups—maybe five, depending on how we group stuff. These four trash groups are plastics, glass, metals, paper/wood, and compostables.

There are the ubiquitous plastics, both soft and hard. Things like buckets, wrappers, and food containers.

There is glass, mostly food and product containers, but also various household glass.

There are the many metals, including food cans, beer cans, old car parts, old tools, screen doors, chain-link fences, and a myriad of everyday objects.

There are paper and wood products, such as wrappers, egg cartons, newspapers, cardboard boxes, books, and many other similar products, most of which biodegrade quickly, and are easily burned.

You could lump fabrics into this last category, though many fabrics are synthetics. These include old clothes, drapes, upholstery, and these too are generally very biodegradable, unless made with synthetics.

Lastly, there are the common items that go into compost pits, such as leaves, food waste, and so on. Since these all biodegrade on their own, and are not particularly useful except as part of the composting process, we won't be addressing them here.

In the aftermath of a disaster, we could be looking at a broad assortment of all these possibilities. But, oddly, in real-life scenarios, you find that though there is always a little bit of everything, there is often an abundance of one or two products, for reasons that can be obvious, or inexplicable.

Let's explore how some of these can fulfill certain needs.

FOOD, COOKING, HEATING

Large soup cans are useful for cooking soups and stews, and purifying water. All hobos know this. You can also invert a large can, cut some smoke holes, turn it upside down, and use it as a makeshift stove in the jungle or backyard.

Sometimes you need a grill or something to get your food away from the fire and not scorched. Any flat piece of metal can work as a grill, even a piece of a car door—but be sure to let it burn a bit so the paint burns off before you start cooking with it.

If you suspend a simple beer or soda can on a tripod over a fire, you can purify water.

A large fifty-five-gallon drum makes a great outdoor space heater. But everyone knows that, right? You all saw Sylvester Stallone in the Lords of Flatbush as the local boys would stand around their fifty-five-gallon- drum fires on cold nights and sing. These drums contain the fire, and make your fire safe.

TOOLS/WEAPONS

In the post-apocalyptic or personal minimalistic world, you will need a personal knife, a large machete-like knife, a shovel, and probably a saw. For a saw, nothing really substitutes, but at least you can make cutting tools and shovels from scrap iron.

The quick makeshift knife is constructed from any flat iron, which you heat and pound into the desired shape. We're not talking esoteric metallurgy here, just the ability to flatten a suitable piece of metal and grind the edge down so it's sharp. Don't bother with a wooden handle in such a situation, but simply wrap the handle with some cordage and tie it off.

TRANSPORT OF WATER

Plastic buckets of various sizes seem to be everywhere, and they are great for washing clothes, storing food, storing water, growing food, making compost, collecting rain, distilling water, and even transporting water. Yes, they really come in handy for water-related issues, something I hope you already knew.

If you have to transport water from the source to your camp, those three- to five-gallon buckets with handles are a great choice. It's even better if they have lids.

Be sure to test how readily you can carry these, because when they have water, they will not be light. Let's say you have "only" three gallons on each bucket. That's six gallons, times about eight-plus pounds a gallon, and you'll have nearly fifty pounds to carry!

WATER PURIFICATION

The easiest way to purify water is to pour it through some cloth, something fine like a pillowcase, and then boil it to make sure it is disinfected. Boil your water in a can.

You can also fill liter water bottles, which are currently a scourge over the face of the earth and are likely to remain so even in the beginning days of post-apocalypse. Lay them in the sun for the UV rays to pasteurize the water.

A simple water still can also be constructed with flat glass or sheets of plastic, and some other hardware. We hope you read up on this before you ever need it, as it's a bit beyond the scope of our simple treatment here.

CLOTHIING

When your clothing wears out, you will (eventually) have to do what everyone else in the history of the world has had to do for clothing:

You go naked or you wear very little, like a loincloth. Or you grow cotton or other plants, process the fibers, loom them into fabrics, and sew that fabric into shirts, dresses, hats, pants, coats, shawls, and whatever you need. Or you kill animals and use their skins to create your garments. In the case of a modern-day minimalist, you can clothe yourself well and at little cost by going to a thrift store and buying clothes. And at some point, you're likely to explore how easy it is to make at least some of your garments. Some garments are complex, and you should have a pattern to follow. Still, with good fabric, scissors, needles, and lots of thread and patience, you can make anything you wear.

We all know that there are about a hundred practical uses for a bandana. Make all the bandanas you need from an old sheet.

In the event of a disaster, clothes will not be a problem initially, but you should start to pay attention so you do not damage your existing clothing more than necessary, and maintain your garments. Should you need simple coats, shirts, or dresses, these are easily made with sheets, blankets, or even upholstery from furniture or cars. If you do not know how to make simple garments, learn. And by "learning," I do not mean watch a YouTube video. Enroll in a junior college class and learn how to size fabric, how to cut it, and how to sew it up by hand to make something you need.

SUMMARY

Everyone's situation is a bit different, whether we're talking about "normal" times or hard times. No one can predict what disasters might befall you, and no one can predict what materials you might have afterwards. Still, we all have the same basic needs, and you'll have to fill those needs with the materials that you have on hand.

Remember: If you find yourself in a post-apocalyptic world, you're not trying to find creative uses for trash; that's what you do at an Earth Day festival. Rather, you're looking for the available trash that will fill your most pressing needs.

An old can is used to purify your water and to cook.

Fifty-five-gallon drums have multiple uses, from stoves, to storage, to a source of scrap metal for makeshift knives and shovels.

A plastic bucket has multiple uses, from a solar still (pictured), to growing food, making compost, and waste disposal.

A plastic liter bottle is good for water storage, and for purifying water in the sun.

Tarps, carpets, and old blankets assist with temporary housing, as urban homeless figured out long ago.

A bandana has about a hundred uses. Proponent for the many uses of the bandana, Francisco Loaiza, shows a bandana printed with survival instructions. A bandana can be cut from an old sheet, shirt, or pillowcase.

PRECEPTS OF MARSHALL GREENWOOD

I first heard of Marshall Greenwood when I read an article about him in the *Los Angeles Times*. He self-described himself as "America's Greatest Poor Man," by choice. I purchased several of his self-published books, and began a long correspondence with him through the US mail in the late 1970s. (He didn't use a telephone so I could not call him, and this was before the days of the internet.)

With his permission, I printed and sold copies of his *Poor Marshall's Manual: The Individual Economics of Living on $99 per Month*. It's an interesting and insightful book by someone who chose minimalism as a more meaningful lifestyle than being a "consumer."

His book consists of four major parts: first, his monthly expenditures; second, his overview and explanation of individual economics; third, how he beats the high price of food; fourth, his laws (173 Precepts) of individual economics; and then an appendix about his fitness regimen.

I'm going to share his expenses (actually, his non-expenses), and just some of the key Precepts. (If you're interested in his full book, check the resources at the end of this book.)

From his preface, he states:

"I seek to glorify the wise, voluntary poverty, which makes the most of the least, shuns folly, conserves the earth's resources, spares the environment, sees (with Aristotle) thinking and reasoning as man's highest function, and pursues learning for its own sake and for the betterment of the world.

"Our consumption-geared economy seeks to:

1. Create need where no need exists.
2. Invent a gadget for every function.
3. Make automatic that which is better manual.
4. Represent costly trivia as necessities.
5. Promote literature, drama, music, and art of dubious merit.
6. Push travel tours that waste earth's dwindling resources, pollute the air, invite crime, spread disease, expose tourists to needless risks, and inflict anguish many times daily on victims who live near airport and approaches, thus shortening their lives…
7. Accelerate consumption of all, leading to misuse, abuse, and premature discard.

"The myriad products of this vigor are displayed as breath-taking opportunities to save. Buyers are depicted in a jubilant scramble to save, save, save. All must be turned on like cheerleaders and jockeyed around like wives at a dude ranch so to be blinded to the obvious, viz., that to save the most is to spend nothing!

"Pursuit of wealth is the folly, the mirage of unenlightened minds. The few who attain great riches in dollars often lament that they did not instead seek learning and wisdom…"

From Part I, MLG Expenditures for one month *[remember, this was 1979]*

Rent, including utilities	$70.00
Food purchases (excluding meat, fish, fowl)	23.67
Food purchases (meal, fish, fowl)	ZERO
Meals eaten out	ZERO
Car, including all related expenses	ZERO
Parking	ZERO
Telephone	ZERO
Newspapers	ZERO
Magazines	ZERO
Shows and concerts	ZERO
Games and sports	ZERO
Cigarettes and cigars	ZERO
Beer, wine, and liquor	ZERO
Haircut and styling	ZERO
Laundromat	ZERO
Cleaning and pressing	ZERO
T.V. repair and depreciation	ZERO
Alterations and mending	ZERO
Boat, camper, R.V.	ZERO
Insurance	ZERO
Doctor bills	ZERO
Dentist bills	ZERO
Hospital expense	ZERO
Classes and lectures	ZERO
Memberships and dues	ZERO
Travels and tours	ZERO
Clothing purchases	1.75
Toilet articles	1.00
Postage, telegrams, delivery	0.04
Food supplements, drugs	1.00
Household supplies and misc.	<u>1.61</u>
1 month total	99.07

Greenwood then offers explanations about this list. In part:

"No mortal can excel the economy of the 24 ZERO budget items.

"I rent a furnished room, twelve feet by fifteen and one-half feet (= 186 square feet), wall-to-wall carpets, with wash basin, hot and cold, two huge windows, good building, twenty-nine units, only two tenants here longer than I.

"Only clothes I ever buy at the store are shorts and sox; all else at rummage, e.g., brand new Arrow dress shirt, 25 cents, new Ben Hogan golf slacks, 75 cents. By inheritance, I got more shoes and sport shirts (all fit) than I can use in my lifetime. I liberated myself from cars in 1955. I walk, run, or cycle; took the bus once in two years. I have all I want. I could trim food bill a bit by cycling afar for super specials, but time is too precious...

"On a half-day's work per week I've done better than others do on six. I owe no one, buy zero on credit. I vote in every election, and without regard for my own interests. I give top priority to my obligations to others....

"Fallacies and ineptitude underlying conspicuous consumption have in misguided minds made wanton waste respectable and frugality miserable. Optimum individual economy requires skill, judgement, intelligence, resourcefulness, patience, discipline."

In his Part III, Greenwood shares some of the ways in which he saves money on food; all of his choices are quality food, with no deprivation. Part of his program is to buy carefully, use coupons, buy on sale, and keep records of all his food consumption. He also describes the thousands of items he gets for free, though he says that he never goes out of his way to find such items. "I'm not a junk man and my time is too precious for such petty profit (such as collecting aluminum cans).... I don't go out to find anything. It finds me. Big difference."

Part IV, the bulk of his book, is titled "Laws of Individual Economics." These are his 173 Precepts, the first group of which are quotes from famous people:

"The cost of a thing is the amount of what I will call 'life' which is required to be exchanged for it immediately or in the long run."
— Thoreau.

"He who is content with contentment is always content." — Laotse.
"To avoid pain, renounce the pursuit of pleasure." — Buddha.

- No set relation obtains among Price, Value, and Quality. Best value can be lowest price, and highest price, or any other… Each case must be decided by itself.
- Ignore any rental ad which omits rent amount.

FOOD CATEGORY

- In eating, a deficit is better than an excess. Great runners have the lean and hungry look.…
- Meat is the worst food one can eat, budget-wise, health-wise, ethics-wise, esthetics-wise, and otherwise.
- Drinking too much water is better than too little. Too much can only irritate. Too little can concentrate urine and possibly cause kidney stones or promote bladder infection. Dehydration poses dangers…
- Best quality and lowest price fruits and vegetables come at season peak. (U.C.Y.?)
- It is a folly to cook dried beans or fresh beets. This takes too long and uses too much fuel. Buy beans and beets in cans.
- Save the liquor from boiled potatoes to make potato soup.
- Rice is the world's most widely used cereal. It is kind to the stomach and colon. Dry rice keeps for years, is easy to cook, and has only 1 percent fat calories of total calories. Boiled cereal digests easier than baked.
- A food which has to be drowned in sugar to be palatable is no good.
- When potatoes are priced high and carrots low, use the latter for the former.
- Taste is a trusty guide of food only in the negative sense, i.e., if it warns that the food is bad, then heed.
- The tastier the food, the less should be eaten; the blander, the more can be safely eaten. Throw away that gourmet book!

DOCTORS CATEGORY

- Cost in money and time of visits to M.D. can be saved entirely in *most* of the following cases (there are exceptions): a. Flu. No treatment is needed. Just bed rest, fruit juice, water, and some extra vitamin C. Two or three days to recover. Ditto for common cold. Penicillin and other antibiotics are no help for these and other viral diseases. Save penicillin for serious bacterial infection. Frequent penicillin impairs effectiveness of shot when really needed….

> *Nationwide statistics were fed into computers in 1972 and it was revealed that 81.7 percent of all illness is self-healing and would "cure itself" if left alone with only bed rest and water.*

APPLIANCES CATEGORY

- The more automatic is an appliance or machine, the more repair it requires….
- Refrigerators, deemed essential, I don't need. My eggs keep okay in north window. None has spoiled in six years; I only use non-fat dry milk and mix only what I use right then. I have no leftovers…
- TV is the most notorious waster of time ever invented. Some persons spend half their waking lives viewing TV's violence, crime, inane sex, stupid commercials, and overdone news (really not *new*, as Thoreau noted)….
- Rent near your work, or get work near where you live. This pays big in dollars and hours … [do the math!].
- A lawn is slavery. Use ice plant or such, or small trees to save much water and work.
- Before rushing to turn on (or up) the room heat, think of Hunza Valley people high in Himalayas who don't heat homes in cold, cold winters and who bathe in cold glacial waters, or, closer to home, think of me who got along just fine in winters with no room heat at all…
- Many drive to a park in order to jog or cycle. Far better is to jog or cycle direct from home and leave car out of it.

- To save gas, ease parking crush, and get needed exercise… cycle or walk all the way [to work].
- Learn to do all needed bike repairs…

MISCELLANEOUS

- Rented storage space, even when dirt-cheap, becomes sky-high in the long run… [do the math: If you are paying $100 a month to store $300 worth of goods, after three months of rental, you could have purchased everything new again. Better to give the goods you cannot store to charity and save the money].
- Costly exercise equipment is largely money wasted since a given exercise with equipment can be equaled or excelled by one sans equipment. Things like exercycles (et al) are zestfully bought, used a few times, then consigned to the dust of the attic.
- Bar toilet soap loses its substance wastefully to wash basin, tub, or shower, as a function of its surface area. To triple life of Ivory bar (and thus triple the dollar), cut into six cubes, put one out at a time till used…
- Don't discard worn bath towel with big hole in the center. Cut off ends for big wash cloths.

SELECT PRECEPTS OF RICHARD WHITE
(covering many categories)

Richard E. White was a Navy veteran, raised in Christian Science, and a lifelong vegetarian. He taught organic gardening, Yoga, and survival training at local schools and colleges. He founded a non-profit, WTI, in order to "Research and share in all aspects of survival, including physical, economic, political, social, and spiritual survival." He also founded a private school, The Rainbow Academy, where he taught numerous curriculums he developed, to the hundreds of students over five decades. He passed away in August of 2019.

This is a general overview, necessarily general, drawn from memory and personal observation. Many of these precepts have evolved into detailed recommendations and procedures, most of which are available from the non-profit that White founded. These are general guidelines that he practiced and taught, and there may be exceptions to the rules in certain cases.

Richard E. White, with Despina Arzouman.

Always first utilize natural methods to heat and to cool rooms and homes.

Never leave lights on when you are not in a room.

Use the most energy-efficient lights.

Use reflectors to increase the light from the bulb.

Don't use electricity if not absolutely necessary.

Use manual tools wherever possible.

If you have an oven pilot light, you can use that to keep warm drinks or soup warm by placing your container over that spot.

White purchased the most energy-efficient refrigerator available at the time, and insulated it with layers of packing bubbles to maintain its insulation. (Refrigerators are perhaps the most inefficient appliance in the modern household.)

A bath is more healthful and efficient than a shower.

All bath water can be recycled into the garden, and some can be bottled to use to flush the toilet.

A few small clothes items can be washed each time you take a bath.

Water heater should be located as close as possible to where the hot water will be used (kitchen sink, bathtub). The water heater tank should be heavily insulated and the lines should be insulated.

Never pay full retail.

Always buy on sale, and with coupons where possible.

Buy in the "off-season" when prices are low.

Buy nothing that you don't actually NEED.

Avoid "impulse buying."

Always find a way, even if you are "poor," to contribute something to a charity or non-profit of your choice.

Do not buy something "on sale" if it is not something you actually use.

Do not "waste" money.

Save 10 percent of your income in the highest interest-bearing account you can find.

Explore real estate and stocks/mutual investments.

Buy in bulk where possible to save money.

Never waste food.

Wear natural fabrics; dress modestly; do not cramp the feet.

Repair your own clothing by learning to sew.

When needing to do home repair and upgrades, always first consider learning some new skills and doing it yourself.

If this is not possible, seek first to hire family, friends, neighbors.

In those jobs requiring specialized knowledge (such as electrical work, or very expensive jobs like installing solar panels, replacing a roof, make room additions, etc.), always get three bids.

Throw nothing away!

Food scraps: Feed to pets, or compost.

Metal pieces: Put in water to rust, and add "iron water" to plants.

Paper: Re-use for letters, typing, notes. Recycle if cannot do that. If very old, feed to earthworms to make soil.

Cardboard: Use for insulation. Use to cover unwanted grasses and weeds in garden, and cover with soil.

Glass: Make cups, chimes, saleable products. Use as molds for candles. Recycle.

Plastic: Reuse where possible. Use for storage. Recycle if possible.

Don't drive a motor vehicle if you can walk or bicycle.

Learn to make simple repairs to your motor vehicle, and to your bicycle.

Learn to help your body heal itself.

Eat nutritious foods. Vegetarianism is best. Grow your own where possible.

Exercise daily with routines that strengthen all systems. (White taught many systems.)

Practice deep breathing. (White taught a system that he called "thorax breathing.")

Practice deep cleaning, with a method such as "entubification."

Lay in the sun with bare skin exposed to get vitamin D.

Fast once a week.

Know your neighbors; join or organize Neighborhood Watch.

Hire your neighbors when you need work done.

Always research new subjects; make discoveries.

Never accept anything because an "expert" says it is so. Do active doubting. Learn by your own direct experience.

Learn new languages. This includes non-spoken languages such as Morse, and sign language.

Constantly refine your own language skills; use a dictionary lavishly. Study *Language in Thought and Action,* by Hayakawa.

Maintain political awareness. Read key books, such as *True Believer* by Hoffer.

Never go to sleep at night without reviewing the day; each night, review each act of importance for what you did right, and what you need to balance.

When you have a need that you need filled, always lead with an offer to the person who might offer assistance. Always look for the way that your offer will be of importance to the offeree.

CHAPTER ELEVEN

OTHER CONSIDERATIONS (Economic and Otherwise)

CLOTHING

People have very specific, and often very peculiar, clothing choices. I cannot help but note the variety of clothing worn by people, though I am very careful to not criticize. Most of us are very conscious of the clothes we wear, and it very much is a part of our self-identity.

I prefer clothing like I prefer art, where form must follow function. This means that your clothing should be made of natural fabrics only, and it should be well-constructed so that it lasts. Your clothing should also be comfortable. Remember, your clothing is your "shelter" at a close distance.

You never want clothing that is harmful to your health or body, or that attracts unnecessary attention to yourself. Clothing that has a lot of loose fringe or other loose segments can get caught in a door or machinery, and might be dangerous. Men's ties are inherently bad because they cut off oxygen flow to the brain. If you must wear a tie, try a clip on. Women's high heels—often considered "hot"—are in fact bad for the spine, and render it impossible to walk—let alone run—properly.

Although camoflauge clothing has become popular, you do not "blend in" in the city environment when wearing camo. Indeed, you stick out like a sore thumb and attract a lot of attention to yourself—which is okay if that's what you want.

CLOTHING QUIZ

Let's see how well you are equipped with the clothing you're now wearing, assuming you'd have to "make it" with just what you are now wearing, for an extended period in the urban wilderness, or even in the outback.

1. Do your pants/trousers restrict your movement due to tightness? ☐ Yes ☐ No
2. Are any of your garments made of polyester? ☐ Yes ☐ No
3. Are any of your garments made of 100 percent cotton or 100 percent wool (or a mix with no more than 20 percent nylon)? ☐ Yes ☐ No
4. Do you have pockets on your shirt/blouse/pants/skirt? ☐ Yes ☐ No
5. Are you wearing any blue clothes? ☐ Yes ☐ No
6. Are you carrying a large kerchief, preferably 100 percent cotton? ☐ Yes ☐ No
7. Are you wearing relatively flat-soled shoes, or high heels? ☐ Flat ☐ High heels
8. Are you wearing shoes comfortable and good-fitting, or much too tight? ☐ Comfortable ☐ Tight
9. Are you wearing a durable leather belt? ☐ Yes ☐ No
10. Are you wearing, or do you have, a hat? ☐ Yes ☐ No
11. Can any of your pockets be closed with buttons, zippers, or Velcro? ☐ Yes ☐ No
12. Are you now carrying a knife? ☐ Yes ☐ No
13. Are you carrying with you some means to start a fire? ☐ Yes ☐ No
14. What is a practical way to double the life of your survival wardrobe?
15. What is the worst fashion item for women?
16. What is the worst fashion item for men?
17. Are you carrying any coin or cash? ☐ Yes ☐ No

You never know if you'll suddenly, and unexpectedly, find your-self in a sheer survival situation. It can happen QUICK and usually it happens when you're least expecting it. Simple attention to your choice of wardrobe—all the time—can help immensely in improving your survival quotient.

ANSWERS

1. "No" is ideal, because tightness restricts movement, and also means that you are getting almost no insulating value from your clothes.

2. "No" is ideal because, in general, polyesters do not "breathe" like natural fibers (cotton, wool, silk). Also, with a few exceptions, polyesters are very poor insulators.

3. "Yes" is the ideal answer because natural fabrics insulate better (though cotton has no insulating value when wet), they "breathe," and they are easier to clean. On the other hand, polyester clothes tend to last longer. Therefore, garments with up to 20 percent polyesters give you added strength that you'd not get with the natural fabric alone.

4. "Yes" is ideal because you can never have too many pockets to carry little things that you need, such as a little knife and a fire starter. Yes, you might carry a pack with many wonderful items, but sometimes it happens that people put down their pack, and somehow, they walk off and never see their pack again. Keep your most necessary essentials in your pockets, or around your neck.

5. "No" is ideal for the one reason that mosquitoes seem to be attracted to blue over any other color. Otherwise, if you are in a dry climate, and nowhere near mosquitoes, it usually makes no difference what color you wear, from a survival standpoint, though there is at least one urban street gang that identifies itself with blue.

6. "Yes" is the ideal answer. There are many uses for that square piece of cotton. For a list of one hundred such uses, see Francisco Loaiza's blog at http://loaizas.blogspot.com/2011/11/uses-for-bandana-first-aid-1.html.

7.   High heels apparently make a fashion statement, and both men and women assert that women look "hot" wearing these shoes. Note, the heel of the foot is pushed up and balanced on a thin rod, upon which the woman must balance her body, working also to maintain spine straightness. Really, objectively, there is not much that's good about the high heel shoe for the woman's body or health. A shoe should be more flat; some heel support can be useful.

8.   This is not too hard to figure out, is it? Yes, obviously, wear comfortable shoes, and not shoes that are too tight for your feet. Shoes that are too tight cut off blood circulation and do not allow for insulation.

9.   "Yes" is the ideal answer. Though a rarity on women's clothing, a belt is useful for carrying a knife, canteen, camera, gun, and many other items. And the belt itself might come in hand for some emergency use.

10. "Yes" is the ideal answer. A hat protects your face and forehead from the sun, and maybe your neck. A hat can also serve to keep your head shaded, and thus cool, in the heat. A hat protects you somewhat from blowing dust.

11. "Yes" is the ideal answer. If you're anything like Tom Sawyer and carry lots of everyday gear in your pockets, you don't want it all falling out if you have to suddenly run somewhere, or climb a rope up a tree, or cross a river.

12. "Yes" is the ideal answer. A knife is part of the "holy trinity" of gear you should always carry. Always!

13. "Yes" is the ideal answer. A firestarter of some sort is another part of the "holy trinity." The ability to make a fire means you can purify water, signal, stay warm, cook food, make tools, dry your clothes, and so much more.

14. This is sometimes debated, and perhaps it depends on the way the garment is made, but if you periodically wear a garment inside out, or backwards where possible, it will wear more evenly, and, theoretically, it will last longer. This is the idea behind "tube socks."

15. High heel shoes, already addressed in number 7.

16. The tie. If too tight, oxygen supply to the brain is limited, which is not a good thing. Also, if you wear a full tie, someone could grab you by it and choke you by the noose you're wearing. If you must wear the silly social custom of a tie, wear a clip-on.

17. Though you might enjoy your life in the city, and your ability to go to the movies periodically, and to wander the aisles of the larger supermarkets with their myriad of supplies, keep in mind that disruptions of various sorts can and do happen all the time. Let's say there's just a minor blackout. That means that most electronic monetary transactions are impossible. You can't use your check or your credit cards or any form of currency that's funneled through your smartphone. However, paper money will usually be accepted, at least in the initial stages of a problem. As time goes on, it's possible that only coin will be accepted for trade.

SEWING SKILLS

One of the best ways to "be prepared" is to always think long-term, not short-term, and always choose quality over the silly fashion whim of the moment. The art of sewing and making your own clothes is a skill that will serve you for your life, in good times and bad.

paper pattern is first used to check for fit. Then e pattern is copied onto fabric, and then cut from e fabric.

Learning how to make a vest. The individual parts were first cut from a pattern, and now they will be sewn together.

If you don't know how to sew, learn! It's not hard. You can take a class at a community college, and there might even be a sewing club in your town. You buy the appropriate fabrics, get a pattern, and then you need scissors, needle, thread, and patience. Lots of guys think they cannot do this because, well, because they are guys! But that's a weak excuse. My mother taught my large family of boys how to sew (and how to cook, also) and it served us well lifelong.

When I have attended local sewing classes to learn a specific technique, I have been the only man there in a room of women. Aside from learning a valuable skill, this is a great place for a man to meet a woman!

GET TO KNOW YOUR NEIGHBORS

"The level of crime in an area is inversely proportionate to the level of communications among the neighbors." — Dave Hereford

Whether you are worried about blackouts, earthquakes, or social unrest for whatever reason, or a comet hitting the earth, your preparedness should begin by getting to know your neighbors. Even if your goal is to live a simple urban life, doing your best to be an ecological model, it still behooves you to get to know your neighbors. Neighborhood Watch forums are ideal ways to have a regular opportunity to exchange phone numbers, meet new folks who have moved into your area, and to share solutions to whatever problems may be impending.

All the guns and dried food and bomb shelters in the world are not as valuable as developing trust and cooperativeness among at least a few neighbors. Remember, in a serious emergency, whoever is living close to you automatically becomes your "extended family"—like it or not, for better or worse.

However, if our neighborhood is any indication of the world at large, you should assume that everyone is busy, no one wants to be the leader, and everyone will wait for someone else. Jump in and take charge. Someone must do it. If you live in earthquake country, take the lead to share "earthquake readiness" skills and "what to store" with neighbors. Then, you can share ideas and information about hurricanes, fires, and literally *whatever* threats your particular community may face.

Get to know who has what skills (doctor, carpenter, plumber, electrician, etc.). Get to know who carries firearms. Since there is so much irrational fear about firearms, perhaps you could form a neighborhood shooting club, and once a month or so go to a local shooting range and practice and socialize. And this should definitely NOT be "just for the guys." Women must become familiar with firearms safety and competence as well. Why? Well, just read the newspapers and the police blotters. Women are frequently the victims, typically assaulted by men, and the out-of-control people in our world *will* take advantage of power outages and emergencies to prey upon the weak and unsuspecting. That is one of the many reasons why the firearm has always been known as an "equalizer."

FAMILY CONSIDERATIONS

If you've actually read this far, you might be thinking, "There are a lot of really good ideas here but, get real, I live in the real world."

Often, an individual will decide that they really want to be a minimalist and live with the barest essentials. And this is very possible, and very fulfilling when you're actually doing it.

But I've observed many times that in family, the father (for example) will say that he works hard to do all these things but the children are too undisciplined to turn off lights after they leave a room. Or that his wife spends too much, and likes to have lots of stuff in the home, which the husband regards as clutter. Or the wife complains that the husband is a slob, and doesn't have the mental discipline to live an ecological life. Spouses blame one another, and they blame their children, and they blame their relatives, and they blame the neighbors, and they blame people they've never even met.

And they are always "right"! I get it. I understand it. Still, I work very hard to not blame anyone for anything that I have chosen to take responsibility for. At the end of the day, you have to make the personal private decision that you want to pursue a lifestyle that has a low carbon footprint, that is ecological, that has as minimal an impact as possible, and that allows you to be a part of the solution to the global commercialization crisis we're surrounded by. Of course, in my case, I'm well aware that such a choice brings with it many detractors, ridiculers, and critics. That's fine. Do it anyway.

ECONOMIC CONSIDERATIONS

One of the essential aspects of self-reliant living—one that we've barely talked about—is economics. It is the white elephant in the room. It permeates everything and every aspect of our decision-making. It is a part of everything we do. It is important to look at the nature of money, and look at our relationship with money, with the same permaculture perspective that we've been looking at everything else.

I'll try to address what I believe are the major topics in as concise a way as possible.

Money—possibly as essential as oxygen in modern society.

WHERE DOES MONEY COME FROM?

Money is a wonderful tool. It is also, in fact, neutral. Money, as we define it in our modern culture, is the result of our collective agreement to have a convenient article of trade so that we can acquire those things we need, and want. Money itself has no value. Most of it doesn't even have intrinsic value anymore, such as the pre-1964 US coins that actually contained valuable amounts of silver. But today it is our agreement that the neutral object of exchange has value, which gives it its practical value. Our agreement is what allows a neutral unit of exchange to have value, and our acceptance that banks and governments can loan it to us is how money is created. That is to say, the creation of debt creates the money. And since banks can lend out more money than they actually have, they are creating money based on the agreement that you will (eventually) pay it back, and then some. Governments do the same. (Yes, I'm aware that "money" based on next to nothing creates a fragile monetary system, and often leads to the collapse of the country's currency—but that's a bit beyond my scope here.)

For our purposes, think of money as a tool. No one actually needs money, per se, but those things and services which money buys. Let that sink in.

Let's talk about earning money, and spending money, and some of our attitudes about money. In our society, everyone needs money. It's about as important as oxygen and good water. So, from childhood we're taught to be good students so we can get a good job so we can get a good pension and retirement plan so we can take care of ourselves in our final years of life before we die. It's never told to us in such a mundane manner, but that's still the message. Learn the skills to be a good worker.

Is that all there is to life? Is that the purpose of life?

If you developed a skill early in life and you were able to obtain employment with your skill, and you were able to provide a home and necessities for you and your family, that is indeed a good thing. If you are self-employed and were able to direct your own destiny, that is ever better, though your challenges and tough times were undoubtedly aplenty.

But perhaps you were not such a person, or because of circumstances beyond your control, and you are now in a situation of examining everything about your life.

Examining how you make money is nearly always a matter of examining your life, because what most people do for most of each day involves getting ready for the job, going to the job, doing the job, getting home, relaxing, thinking about the job, etc. Often, our job is our life. And yes, I understand the necessity at times to do anything, anything, anything to make an income so you're not homeless, hungry, and humiliated in a money-focused society.

Okay, let's just get very basic. This may or may not apply to you, but the principles are sound. When you need more money, you can sell something you have, which will be a product or a service. You can borrow, but that is an avenue of last resort usually.

MAKE A LIST

When I have been in this position, I would make a list of everything that I could sell immediately, or within a reasonable time. Then, I list how precisely I can sell those items, and then I begin taking action on at least the top three most likely salable items on the list. Often, this produces the income I need.

Then, I make a list of any service I can offer to someone, based on some talent I have developed. The list has to be realistic, services that I know someone would pay for. As an adult, I am not going to try and sell lemonade on the street corner. Plus, I do not consider any illegal services. Just services that provide a need or solve a problem. Then, for each of those services, I list precisely how I will market that skill, and to whom. Often, to get some quick results, I get on the phone and begin calling my contacts, one by one. And I never call and say, "Hey look Jim, I am really down on my luck and I am hoping you can hire me to do a complete detail job on your car…." That might work, based on pity, but a better option is find the reason that your service will benefit your potential employer, and emphasize only the benefit to him or her when you call. In other words, "Jim, this is your lucky day. I'm not far from you today and I can do a top-rate professional detail job on your car for less than any of those big boys doing it, and I can come to you!" Or whatever the skill is that you're offering, your job before even making the phone call is to find out what your potential employer *needs* and then *lead with an offer* when you call. People are far more inclined to work with you when they see that you're not just worrying about yourself (even if you're actually panicking), but actually concerned about their welfare. I know this works because I have done it many times.

But don't overlook taking the time to review your own skills and talents, and to actually write down a list. You might be surprised at your own hidden talents that you've not been bringing to the fore. Maybe it's time to write a new resume.

Once you start to get your personal cash flow flowing again, do not become complacent. Be the type of person that anyone would want around, a problem-solver, a pro-active doer who doesn't wait to be told.

WHEN SHOULD YOU BORROW?

Should you ever borrow money to get out of financial trouble? In general, the answer is no. The only three big purchases that are acceptable to go into debt to purchase are an education, a house, and maybe a vehicle. A business is another possibility.

The problem with getting hooked on credit cards is that it is too easy to get hooked on them. Borrowing the money will relieve your problems temporarily and you might even feel proud that you are "only" paying a low interest rate. But if you haven't solved the issue of earning money, the debt just grows larger and larger.

I remember a friend telling me that he had a certain amount of money left to spend. I asked him what he meant by that. "I only have $300 of credit left that I can spend," he explained. In other words, he'd already spent all the allowable credit on his card, and he was within $300 of his credit limit.

"You don't have any money left," I told him. "You're not describing any money that's yours. That $300 is how much more the bank is allowing you to go further into debt!"

My friend told me that "you just don't get it," and stormed off.

Do whatever you can to stay out of credit card debt, and one way to do this is to analyze each and every purchase you are contemplating.

Ask yourself these questions:

Why can't I just pay for this item with cash? If you cannot afford to pay for it with cash, this means, simply, you cannot afford it!

Will this item allow me to earn more income? Sometimes, if you buy something that increases your net income—something that you can resell for more, or something that allows you to do a job—that could be acceptable. But if you are just buying something that you don't really need, something that you just "like," then it's probably something that you can live without, and you should not buy it.

Even though money is a neutral tool that has no intrinsic value, you should still treat it like a treasure and not waste it. The easy ability to buy with credit, and "pay later," allows us to think too casually about money and to waste money on the things we do not actually need.

Consider: When you sell something for a profit, for money, and when you are paid in money for a job you've done, you have effectively traded your most valuable asset—your time—for the neutral unit of exchange. Thus, the neutral unit of exchange represents your time, meaning, it represents your life!

When you consider what you want your life to be all about (and this is regardless of your current age), you might reconsider some of the ways in which you deal with money.

I encourage you to treat your money as if you'll live to 100, and do the wisest investing and saving that's possible for you. How to handle your money has been handled in great depth by many other authors.

When thinking about the choices we make that relate to money, I am reminded of a lecture series I presented many years ago at the WTI monthly Plenary gatherings. The lecture was called "The Four Illusions of Money." Here are some highlights.

FOUR ILLUSIONS OF MONEY

The WTI Plenary sessions were all-day seminars where participants shared specific research in the areas of politics, economics, nutrition, history, and more. I had been giving presentations on money-related topics, such as "What is money?," "What is the Federal Reserve?," "What is the IMF," and others.

The money-related lecture that stirred up the greatest emotional response was "The Four Illusions of Money." My presentation was loosely based on an article with the same name that appeared in the winter 1979–80 issue of *Co-Evolution Quarterly*. The presentation and discussion lasted about two hours, covering many facets and dealing with the comments and objections from the audience. Here is a condensation of that presentation.

When people are queried, almost everyone says that they do not have enough money, and would like to have more. Furthermore, one of the most commonly cited reasons given by people who continue to work at a job they dislike is to "make a lot of money." The reasons that this is such a ubiquitous goal—to make a lot of money—can be summed up in the four following rationales:

1. A lot of money will let me be free to do what I want to do.
2. People with a lot of money command more respect from others.
3. I need more money for my family.
4. Money is necessary for my security in old age.

Yes, there are many more such "illusions" that dance around money, but these four seemed to fairly concisely address all the secondary and corollary illusions.

These four statements are illusions about money. That means, these represent false perceptions of the world. In other words, when we embrace any or all of these four illusions, we are prevented from seeing the NON-monetary realities about our life and the choices that we make.

Let's explore these one by one.

A lot of money will let me be free to do what I want to do.

One way to see through this illusion is to make a specific list of all your carefully considered goals. These can be short-term and long-term goals. These can include travel, projects, achievements, possessions, skills (learning a new language), etc., but the list cannot include money. Money cannot be a goal. Next, you should examine the list you made and begin to delineate precisely how you can go about achieving that goal.

Yes, of course, money can help accelerate the achievement of the goal. Still, once your goals are clearly established in your own mind—and clearly differentiated from "passing wants"—you can steadily move forward, step by step, toward the achievement of that goal. Money is incidental to this process, and must not be allowed to determine the choices you make and the steps that you take.

A large part of achieving a goal—perhaps the most important part—is to learn valuable life-enhancing skills that you wouldn't have learned otherwise.

And many of the essential steps toward a goal involve working with other people. Working with other people develops strong friendships and relationships, and this requires that you must be—or must become—reliable and trustworthy yourself. This manner of pursuing and achieving goals should represent a true freedom from our enslavement to money, and should open you up to some truly life-enhancing experiences.

Remember, this perspective is offered as an alternative to "going out to make enough money so I can be free to do what I want to do."

One of the amazing insights that I gained while sharing this at our seminar was how many people actually had no clearly defined goals at all.

People with a lot of money command more respect from others.

This is demonstrably and abundantly false. There is no reason to believe that people with "a lot" of money automatically command genuine respect (in fact, they don't), or that people with "a lot" of money command respect *because* of the money.

People who invite respect do so because of their personal qualities, talents, character, and experience. It may be the case that these very qualities are the reasons why a person has been able to earn "a lot" of money. But money itself is not the basis for real respect.

How do I know this? Look at what happens to those who claim respect for someone when the money is gone.

Just try the following experiment for yourself. Make a list of twenty-five people whom you respect. These must be people that you know personally and you interact with in some way, not just people that you know about from the TV or newspapers. Do your best to attempt to "score" how much you respect them, using a system for example of listing each from one to one hundred, one hundred being the highest level of respect. Next, do your best to list the income (or net worth) of each of the individuals on your list. In cases of genuine respect, you will rarely find a correspondence between how much you respect that person and how much money they make.

An observation. Most people at my talks were able to write a list of the top twenty-five people they respected. Most had the list written in under five minutes. Then, the scoring of each person from one to one hundred generally took another five minutes. When we did this at a seminar, we'd wait until everyone had their lists written before proceeding. One of the things that we learned from this, when we had the means to verify the income amounts, was that 1) most "friends" were quite "in the dark" about how much money the people they respected earned. Usually, they overestimated. And 2), as we already stated, those who were believed to earn the most money were not the ones who were at the top of the "respect list."

I need more money for my family.

All too often, people use this fallacy as an excuse for doing something they would rather not do. This rationale is especially typical of "bread-winners" who work extra hours and on weekends so they can pay for possessions and vacations that they believe their family needs and deserves.

If you are getting more and more out of touch with your own family members because you are spending more and more time away from them supposedly so you can provide something more for them, then you are falling for this illusion.

It would be far more valuable for everyone if these bread-winners instead spent valuable time with their family members, and finding a way to re-orient the job and financial choices.

Sometimes the most valuable time spent with one's children is the time spent to teach and work with them to develop their own businesses.

As for the myth of "quality time" over "quantity of time," don't believe it! Your notion of "quality time" means very little to young people. The best way to have quality time is to assure that you have sufficient time together.

Money is necessary for my security in old age.

I had barely spoken these words in my seminar presentation when the groans and loud objections were voiced. Two men got into an argument over this point before I'd barely gotten started, and I had to tactfully break it up. Yes, we have a lot of baggage about money, and getting older doesn't make this any better.

Money is needed in many ways, of course, but personal security, inner and outer, cannot be purchased.

The real security that is most needed by elderly people can be enhanced by money, but it can never be built solely upon money. Inner security arises with the development of deep friendships, and with learning to be flexible and adaptable, for example, and these are not things that are in any way dependent upon money.

In fact, one of the best ways to "prepare for old age" is to become the type of person—inwardly and outwardly—that other people will want to be around and work with.

This means being competent, helpful, flexible, honest, moral, curious, always willing to learn and to share, generous, and so on. And note that none of these virtues are either the intrinsic or exclusive virtues of the wealthy.

Developing one's character is clearly one of the best ways to prepare for the calamities that might strike any of us at any age, such as wars, depressions, social chaos, as well as a whole host of personal difficulties.

The discussion went on for another hour—heated at times—and fortunately no chairs or windows were broken.

LEARN TO PRODUCE

History has also taught us that those who learn to produce what they need, and then do so, are invariably more free than their neighbors who do not do so. There are exceptions of course, but those who grow their own food can then sell the surplus of what they grow for the cash to buy what they cannot barter.

In a famous discussion between Merlin and King Arthur (yes, I know I am stretching it a bit here), Merlin told his student that there would never be war if people chose to be self-sufficient.

The way to apply these simple principles tends to be complex, and always further complicated by politicians who are lost in their worlds of words. Still, freedom to do what is right should be the goal of everyone.

And despite all the bickering and fighting that still continues to this day over what the US is and what it represents, I find that the best rule of thumb for guidance is the Golden Rule: "Do unto others as you would have them do unto you."

From a Navajo basket-maker, from a television documentary:
"My mother told us that if we could make something, and sell it, we'd never be poor.
We'd never be rich either (laughter), but we'd never be poor."

WHAT DID I LEARN FROM THIS?
List three of your goals.

List three ways to work towards EACH of those goals, and you may not list "money" as one of the methods.

EDUCATION

It's amazing to me how often people I encounter have told me that they no longer read books, study, or take classes because "I graduated from school a long time ago." Amazing!

Exercising and expanding the mind is equally (if not more so) important than exercising the body lifelong. Everyone seems to intuitively know that you always need to maintain the health of the body with exercise, good diet, cleanliness, and so on. Why then should we stop exercising the mind?

Going to school is great, and all children should be strongly encouraged by their parents to finish high school, and at least two years of college.

I loved sitting in a classroom and learning. The hardest part was the distance, when the school was across town, and, of course, the price. We've all heard that education is expensive, but that ignorance is even more expensive. True. But keep in mind that education can come to you in many forms.

Whether you have a regular job, are self-employed, or work at home, you should constantly find ways to learn more—not just to "make money," but to enrich your mind, and quality of life.

This includes reading very selective books, and ideally making notes and questions as you go along.

This includes taking classes at the community college, attending lectures, and taking online classes. To expand the mind, you must be a proactive student and constantly ask questions, take notes, and create experiments so you can test your new learning.

The key to real learning lies in two factors: 1. The quality of the teacher, and 2. Your desire to do the work required to learn the subject matter. Thus, the fact that you spent a lot of money for tuition and travel to the very well-regarded college does not guarantee that your "learning" will be life-enhancing nor worthwhile. Nor, on the flip side, should you discount the immense value that you could derive from a lecture at the local library. The only thing that really matters is the quality of the information—which is up to you to ultimately verify—and the persistence and quality of your own study and follow-up research.

TELEVISION

I read *Four Arguments for the Elimination of Television*, by Jerry Mander, and there were good points made. Mindless television watching, or watching for casual entertainment, is a time waste, bad for your health, and counterproductive.

In my interactions with Richard White, to whom I dedicated this book, he encouraged all his new students to regard television as a unique learning tool which had to be used very carefully and specifically in order for them to derive real and lasting benefits.

In my first semester at his peripatetic school, I recall that he asked us to look at the miracle of television, and to explore the meaning of that word: Tele—from afar, and Vision—seeing. That is, "seeing from afar." In the last many thousands of years, we aren't aware of any other humans who had the benefit of "seeing from afar" news, educational material, insightful drama, and insight into the world in which we live. To drive home this sense of awe, White always referred to the television as "the far-seeing magic lantern."

Yes, he quickly pointed out much of what is transmitted over the television is designed to keep us sitting there so we can watch the sponsor's advertisements to buy things that we probably do not need. And then, the overwhelming bulk of what's transmitted is what White referred to as "Yok, sock, and diddle," meaning, inane comedy, fighting, and sex, in various guises and combinations.

Yet, there is still value within the vast television transmissions if you work to seek them out.

Here is a summary of some of the ways he encouraged us to use television.

Take college-level courses from TV. (This has largely been replaced by online education.) Under the guidance of White, most of his students enrolled in local community college courses that could be taken by watching the classes on TV, and then going to the college for a midterm and final exam.

Public TV generally had the best shows for in-home learning, covering in an objective and no-nonsense manner such topics as economics, nutrition, the natural environment, ecology, politics, human nature, human relations, and so on.

Find and view the most objective interview shows. Observe the techniques of the good interviewer for drawing out information.

In cases of "fictional" shows, actively look for the universal lesson.

White had a long list of shows that conveyed key lessons worth learning. On some occasions, we'd watch a show and the discussion would last longer than the show. Some very few examples in no particular order: "Burmese Harp," David Carradine's "Kung Fu" pilot, "Shawshank Redemption," "It's A Wonderful Life," "The Killing Fields," "Year of Living Dangerously," "Gandhi," "Being There," and countless others. When we gathered as a class, we'd view the show, pause it often for commentary, and then discuss the valuable lessons that we should apply in our lives, as well as the points that were less useful, and best ignored.

When watching TV, don't sit lazily. Keep the body in a strengthened posture, or do exercises while you view.

Take notes on key points; verify facts you're uncertain about.

Write articles based on your insights from particular shows.

Do mundane tasks while viewing, such as weaving/ knitting, cleaning small objects, and so on.

Richard White was very much the ultimate permaculturalist in the broadest sense, even utilizing TV as a learning tool, where one did not need to rush on the road and freeways to some distant building to take a class, but one could actually make a dynamic personal move-ahead by proactively utilizing the tool of the "far-seeing magic lantern."

In a sense, the computer has replaced the television, and much of this is now taken for granted. However, it should be noted that another extreme has developed where individuals are "make-believe" learning something by watching everything on YouTube. As long as there is actual application being practiced, real learning can take place.

LASTLY....

According to Jane Jacobs, author of *Dark Age Ahead,* Western societies are following the same cultural decline that occurred with the Roman Empire. She tells us that dark ages are a lot more common than we may think, and she identifies many of the weak spots in our contemporary lifestyle.

Her list of weak areas includes all of the obvious: taxes, family, community, education, science, technology, the lack of self-policing, and moral/ethical insanity.

Jacobs believes that these weak areas are the foundation of all the other often-cited problems, such as the environment, crime, and the discrepancy between rich and poor.

Jacobs insightfully points out that modern families are "rigged to fail" due to rising housing prices, suburban sprawl (with a reduced sense of community), and the automobile. She regards the automobile as the chief destroyer not only of communities but of the *idea* of community. Think about that one! When you are able to walk or bicycle through your community, you get to know it so much better.

Jacobs is hopeful, and does not see dark ages as inevitable. She suggests that we all need to get involved and be a part of the solution. Jacobs points out that the millions of details of a complex, living culture are not transmitted via writing or pictorially, but by (1) living examples and (2) word of mouth. Jacobs goes on to say that though "the end" may be near, there are things we can do. What are those actions?

We need to think.

We need to model solutions.

We need to teach, to lecture, and to write.

Each of us has the potential to be a part of the solution to the greater problems facing us all, and that means that we engage in our society in an uplifting and meaningful way.

Bicycling can have a profound effect on creating a sense of community. Outdoor educator Ed Parker bicycles nearly every day of the year.

CHAPTER TWELVE

A SIX-STEP PLAN TO ADDRESS CLIMATE CHANGE

Six simple solutions that anyone can implement locally in their own backyards.

Shawn Maestretti, a landscape architect, arborist, and contractor, shares data on climate change in his lecture series, as well as how these changes can affect our landscape.

Though his engaging program focuses on how an individual can be a part of the solution and make a positive effect in their own garden, his presentation begins with the "big picture." Maestretti shows pictures of Earth from space, and explains how the first Earth Day began when we realized that it wasn't a good idea to use our atmosphere as an open sewer for unwanted gases. "Currently, 110 million tons of manmade pollution goes into this thin shell of our atmosphere, our space," he told the audience.

He pointed out that though agriculture is a contributor of CO_2 into space, agriculture can also be a solution, through regenerative agriculture. The main source of CO_2 in space is the burning of fossil fuels.

To put this in historical perspective, he points out that there has always been a contraction and expansion of CO_2 in the environment, over long periods of time, but it has never gone over 300 ppm annually. "We did that as of 2013," he explains.

"We must make dramatic changes during the next forty years," says Maestretti. "If the increase of CO_2 emissions continues to steadily increase, it will be hard to be outside."

Maestretti explains that we have solutions, but we need to choose to implement them. He says that we need to have zero waste, reduce CO_2 emissions, and look to nature for solutions.

He lays out a six-part program of regenerative practices that anyone can practice in their own yard. Here is the bare-bones overview of Maestretti's six points, which he expands upon in his programs.

NURTURING THE LIVING SOIL

Maestretti next to backyard composters, which are one of the simplest ways to recycle yard leaves and kitchen scraps and create quality soil.

Maestretti explains that all life starts with the soil, and we have to work harder to regenerate the soil. Tilling destroys topsoil where the organic matter resides, and releases carbon into the atmosphere. He spends significant time describing the makeup of soil, and how everything should be done to avoid erosion and the destruction of such life forms as the fungi in the soil, which help to increase soil fertility. Unfortunately, modern agricultural and urbanization practices are turning the land into deserts. By poor agricultural practices, about a third of arable land on Earth has been lost in the last thirty years.

"It's not drought that causes bare ground," says Maestretti. quoting Allan Savory. "It's bare ground that causes drought." Thus, he's a proponent of protecting the topsoil through mulching and other methods.

OPTIMIZING WATER USE

In the urban setting, most people are able to capture rainwater into drums or cisterns, by capturing it off their roofs. That water should be used in the yard, and not sent to the ocean down the storm drains. Water should also be optimized by planting appropriate natives that don't require as much water.

LAND FORMS/ HÜGELKULTUR

Maestretti recommends that people build berms and swales so the water that does flow through your land actually stays there and soaks in. This is the principle behind the settling ponds that you see in many communities, which allows the water to soak into the local water table rather than quickly flowing to the ocean.

Maestretti shows a simple method to capture rainwater in one's own urban and suburban yard.

Prunings and especially old wood can be buried into the berms, capture and store moisture, and they gradually decompose and add nutrients to the soil—a technique known as "hügelkultur." This allows the carbon from those wood and leaf prunings to go back into the soil, adding moisture and nutrients.

PERMEABLE GROUND

Maestretti encourages the removal of, and reduction of, unnecessary blacktop or cement. There are currently numerous products that allow the water to soak into the soil, such as blocks that can actually be driven on that have holes where grass can be grown and water can soak in.

Maestretti next to tree prunings and chips, which will be used in a berm at his small urban demonstration plot.

There are, for example, cement blocks with decorative holes that can be laid down in place of solid cement. A car could drive on this, but water would still soak into the ground. This has become so "mainstream" that you can find products of this type at most home-improvement big box stores.

PLANTING FOR SOIL AND HEALTH

According to Maestretti, plants are the key to our salvation. They draw carbon out of the atmosphere, and without the trees and plants, there would be much more evaporation of water, compaction of the soil, and run-off. In both farming and backyard landscaping, he encourages both green and brown mulch. Brown mulch is temporary, and includes such things as wood chips and ground compost that keeps moisture in the soil. Green mulch refers to growing such plants as clover and other groundcovers, which impact the small water cycle by slowing evaporation and continually enriching the soil.

"Remember," exclaims Maestretti, "that plants allow us to eat sunlight." There was a bit of silence in the room as the audience pondered this fact.

PLANTING FOR BIODIVERSITY AND HABITAT

In the complex web of life, insects are the link between plants and all higher creatures in the food chain, and we should keep that in mind when we plan and implement our gardens. We need not focus on killing off all insects. Diversity builds strength into the garden.

Maestretti's goal is to encourage everyone to play a role in being the solution to the global change we're experiencing. This can be done

Shawn Maestretti in his yard where he conducts workshops.

somewhat painlessly, by the way we work with the land under our control. His vision is that any average lot can be a solution with wild and cultivated plants, where all the rain that falls there is captured, where all the prunings and wood from the plants there are returned to that land's soil. Not only does he conduct workshops to show homeowners how to accomplish these regenerative tasks, but he also practices what he preaches in his own yard.

"Besides all the obvious benefits of a garden, remember that such a garden cools the environment. In fact," added Maestretti, "plants actually cool our cities."

Shawn Mestretti is a landscaper, landscape architect, arborist, contractor, Kiss the Ground Soil Advocate, and a member of the Climate Reality Leadership Corp. He can be reached at shawn@smgarchitecture. com, www.smgarchitecture.com.

CHAPTER THIRTEEN
FINAL COMMENTS

To engineer a sustainable city, we must re-engineer our thinking.

A tipi in the hills of Los Angeles, showing that low-tech can live side-by-side with high-tech.

Growing up in a suburb of Los Angeles, I did not have an immediate knowledge of where our food and water came from. I turned on the faucet for water, plugged cords into the wall for electricity, and went to the store for food. Yes, my city had been engineered for me, and I was just mindlessly playing my role.

At a young age, I felt that there was something wrong with my ignorance. Even worse, no one else seemed to be aware of our unawareness. Everything came from *somewhere else.* One salvation for me was that my mother grew up on a farm, and would tell tales of the Great Depression and the Dust Bowl, where many people had no food, and some starved to death. My mother's family was poor by most standards, but they had fifty-one acres in rural Ohio and they fed themselves and many others. My mother's stories inspired me to become an ethno-botanist, and to learn about how all plants were used in the past.

Though I did not pursue the path of "urban planning," and knew I would never be engineering my city or any city, I realized that I had many choices within the framework of my suburban life where I could ecologically engineer *my* life.

PERSONAL CHOICES

My first teenage forays were into backyard urban gardening and raising chickens in a tiny space. I didn't want to be dependent on commercial fertilizers and bug sprays, so I learned the ages-old methods of agriculture, methods that people today call "organic" or "permaculture." I learned that anyone could indeed produce at least some of their food in a small amount of space.

A 1974 newspaper article showing Christopher demonstrating organic gardening when he was still in his teens. The garden was a small urban plot.

Even in my late teenage years, I had critics who told me it was not practical to grow foods without artificial fertilizers and pesticides. Really? I followed the path of Fusuoka and his "One Straw Revolution," and the Rodale family, and insisted on growing everything with nothing artificial. I learned to keep down the bug population with natural methods that had been practiced worldwide for millennia. I knew that the so-called Green Revolution, based as it was on petroleum-based fertilizers and pesticides, was partly a fraud, and was not sustainable into the future centuries.

I continued my botanical studies by learning about the uses of wild plants by the Native Americans. I found to my surprise that all the foods used by the indigenous population could still be found throughout my homeland, though it was necessary to hunt a bit more because of all the houses, roads, and modern landscaping that has taken over the land. Yes, the engineering of the concrete city had destroyed much of the territory for these native foods, but they were not entirely gone.

Nyerges teaches urban dwellers how to recognize useful wild plants in the wild places around the city.

I began to eat these wild plants that had sustained people for millennia, and I incorporated them into my regular diet. When I first began to share my excitement of these floral treasures with others, I was treated with mostly apathy, sometimes scorn, and even pity. I was amazed!

Nyerges leads a wild food walk in what appears to be a wilderness area, but is actually in the city.

RE-ENGINEERING MY OWN MIND

In the mid-1970s, in Los Angeles County, I began publicly teaching and writing about the practical skills of self-reliance and practical survival *in the city* I was working to engineer a new mindset that says we can live ecologically (and economically) in a city.

Today, there is a renaissance and a great interest in the knowledge of our ancestors. And it's never too late to begin to seek our roots, and to turn around some of habits of ecological suicide. I believe that we can solve many of our problems today by looking to the past for some of our solutions.

Here in southern California, politicians and water department movers and shakers have finally begun to encourage the millions of people who live here to consume less water. With water usage averaging about 131 gallons a day for Los Angeles residents, and an ever-growing population of about 5 percent a year, water must always be a concern, as it will always be for most major cities of the world.

The mayor of Los Angeles, and water department officials, are encouraging people to tear out their lawns and install drought-tolerant plantings. I encourage people to go even one step further. Actually, a few steps further. Yes, learn about the wild plants which are edible and medicinal, and encourage them. They will grow without your care. And never merely plant "ornamentals"—that is, plants that do not provide food, medicine, or good mulch from their leaves. Plant with a purpose to feed your body and your soul.

Nyerges shows carrots from his small backyard garden. Photo by Helen Nyerges.

To help irrigate these useful plants, I'm a big proponent of simple grey-water recycling, where your sink and washing machine water are piped into your backyard garden or front-yard orchard. Not every city dweller can do this, but enough can do it to make a large difference. Yes, certain changes are essential, such as buying soaps that contain no dyes, colors, or

A garden can be grown in any small area, as illustrated in this small front-yard garden.

harmful chemicals. Continuing education is a big part of self-reliance and sustainability. Recycling your grey water means that you are getting at least two uses from water that previously you used only once. Practically speaking, for every gallon of water you recycle, you have effectively created another gallon of water for your use that does not have to be imported from somewhere else.

With the population of southern California that continually grows, there is the growing need for more food and more water, as a function of increased population. This unfortunately means even more land paved over for more houses or apartments. Thus, the very soil which all ancient civilizations knew was the foundation of a healthy society becomes more and more rare. This should not be the case, even though it seems all but inevitable.

Our very lifeblood is dependent on the soil in so many ways: water, food, everything. However, urban people need to re-learn these very basic ecological principles. Our very laws, and attitudes—especially in the more "developed" countries—work against our long-term sustainability.

This is a neighborhood garden, found in many cities, where you can rent a plot and grow vegetables.

scar Duardo runs a neighborhood garden not far from downtown os Angeles. He is standing next to an amaranth patch.

An urban front yard that has been converted into an herb garden.

URBAN SUSTAINABILITY

The green lawn is still the norm in the sprawling suburban flatlands. Never-ending flows of water (from somewhere) is the expectation. The mindset must turn around, and it will begin with enlightened

Kevin Sutherland examines a rain collection system in an urban front yard. The system includes eleven of these old pickle barrels.

individuals who see that inappropriate lifestyles in an over-populated dry terrain are the antithesis of survival. As attitudes change—and slowly they are—the laws of the land need to support the water-wise practices that support sustainability.

I cringe when I see television advertisements for such products as Roundup, and others, designed to kill off the unwanted vegetation of urban gardens and landscapes; you know, such plants as dandelions and other healthful herbs called "weeds" that they picture in their ads.

Support your local farmers, markets, where you can buy locally produced fruits and vegetables.

To me, a student of the wild plants and the things growing in the faraway and neglected places, using a chemical like Roundup to "clean up" a wild area is a sacrilege. Further, bankers and land investors do not necessarily see the land as a source of life, recreation, fulfillment, and community. Rather, increasingly, the desire is to extract the greatest financial benefit from the land. Land that has nothing built upon it is all too often described as "non-performing real estate." That is the mentality which has caused the urban sprawl to sprawl even farther, while diminishing the very sustainability from the land that we all need. "Engineering" the city should not be simply building ever-more structures on the diminishing landscape. We should be re-engineering our thinking so we can get more from less, in ways that are both healthful and ecological.

THE QUIET REVOLUTION

I am a pioneer of the path of the green and sustainable revolution. You won't find me protesting in the streets for changes, but you might find me in a city council meeting. I work with people one at a time. I have found that once an individual sees that the so-called weeds in an empty field are actually great nutritious food or medicine, they suddenly take a very personal interest in protecting and caretaking the land.

Once individuals learn that the water from their very households can water their own garden and herb patch, they become quite alert and aware of the quality of any soaps they are using, and they begin to use only those that are biodegradable, as a result of enlightened self-interest. Suddenly, living an ecological urban life becomes very personal.

There are many paths to urban sustainability. This is the path I have chosen. If we all work together and make a commitment to this common goal, the world can be a wonderful place.

READING LIST AND RESOURCES

GENERAL URBAN SUSTAINABILITY

Extreme Simplicity: Homesteading in the City, Christopher and Dolores Nyerges

Self-Sufficient Home: Going Green and Saving Money, Christopher Nyerges

Living Like Ed: A Guide to the Eco-Friendly Life, Ed Begley Jr.

One Straw Revolution: An Introduction to Natural Farming, Masanobu Fukuoka

SURVIVAL SKILLS

Survival Skills of Native California, Paul Campbell

How to Survive Anywhere, Christopher Nyerges

Enter the Forest, Christopher Nyerges

Testing Your Outdoor Survival Skills, Christopher Nyerges

HISTORICAL

House of Rain, Craig Childs

PLANT IDENTIFICATION

Guide to Wild Foods and Useful Plants, Christopher Nyerges. This book covers the edible and useful plants throughout the US, with all color photos.

Foraging Edible Wild Plants of North America, Christopher Nyerges. This book covers the most common wild foods throughout the US, with lots of recipes, and full-color photos.

Healing with Medicinal Plants of the West, Dr. James Adams, Abedus Press.

HOW TO STORE FOOD

Stocking Up, Carole Rupping, Rodale Press. This is a classic book on how to dry, freeze, can, etc.

CULTURAL CONSIDERATIONS

Language in Thought and Action, S. I. Hayakawa. This is the *the* book for "how to think." If you've not read *and studied it,* get it today from a used book store.

The Art of Loving, Eric Fromme. In the classic book on the problems facing all of humanity, Fromme describes the science of love. This book teaches you "how to love."

True Believer, Eric Hoffer. The quintessential book on mass movements and cults teaches you "how to believe."

Man and Woman and Child, Harold W. Percival. This is perhaps *the* most important book on who and what we are, and what is our ultimate destiny.

Democracy Is Self-Government, Harold W. Percival. A "must-read" if you are to grasp what's wrong with modern politics. The author demonstrates that individual self-government is the only path to real democracy.

APPENDIX

From the *Pasadena Star-News*, 1971, by staff writer Wayne Harpe.
Reprinted with permission.

Organic Gardener Provides Feast from One-Acre Plot
Think you have to pack your bags and move to an Arizona commune to enjoy the "fruits of nature"? You're wrong. Organic gardener Richard White has found that fruits and a variety of foods grow quite well on his one-acre lot on Burwood Terrace in Highland Park.

White often awakes to consume two eggs, green vegetables, corn on the cob, and coffee for breakfast.

Unlike most area residents, White's feast was not purchased at the local grocery, but grown organically.

His eggs are from chickens raised on yard-grown grain and vegetables. His naturally sweetened corn is plucked minutes before it is to be eaten, warmed and served. His dandelion greens, usually prepared rare, are unrecognizable from spinach or mustard greens when cooked. His coffee is strained and sweetened with raw sugar before being consumed.

Although White lives with his wife, Monika, on a hilltop in near seclusion, he is far from a hermit. He shares his knowledge with others.

Special classes, open to the public, are conducted each week, at his home and on the campus of Pasadena City College. White has been unsuccessful in his attempts to get the class accredited. PCC officials said he lacked the necessary credentials.

"One aim," he says, "is to develop people who could go out and survive on their own, if need be during a depression, using natural chemicals alone."

He says regular fertilizers are composed primarily of nitrogen, potash, and phosphorus. Minute trace elements, essential for healthy crops and found abundantly in nature, are absent. Scientists have failed to duplicate them and many remain unknown.

"Soil preparation is the worst tragedy," says White. "The regular farmer gets away from natural development. When nature plants a seed, does it ever turn the soil over?"

Nutrient-saturated soil yields healthy plants which repel disease and insects without the aid of pesticides, he says. Conventional plants, grown in depleted soil, invite insects and ailment.

Compost, a homemade fertilizer, is the major problem facing organic farmers. Compost must be prepared and layered correctly or rodents, which spread disease, may be attracted to it, he says.

White's homemade fertilizer is piled in an eighteen-inch by eighteen-inch hole, nearly two feet deep just outside the house. The material was watered once, in the beginning, then covered with an old soaked blanket to trap moisture. The water had previously been used to wash the dishes.

Five weeks later the material had decomposed, collected bugs and other organisms that add nutrients and turned into moist, rich dirt.

After decomposition, compost is removed from the hole and used as top soil. Mulch, weeds, leaves, ground wood, and "almost anything" is periodically placed around the crops to aid nourishment.

White has an assortment of plants—rose hips, mustard greens, bamboo shoots, wild wheat, berries—all growing in his unconventional garden. The plants, unbound by neatly stacked rocks or fencing, thrive throughout his yard wherever room permits.

ABOUT THE AUTHOR

Christopher Nyerges works to engineer a new mindset that says we can live ecologically (and economically) in the city. He has taught self-reliance and sustainability his entire life through the teaching of ethnobotany and principles of permaculture. Nyerges is the author of nineteen books, including *Self-Sufficient Home: Going Green and Saving Money, Extreme Simplicity: Homesteading in the City, How to Survive Anywhere*, and others. He is the founder of the School of Self-Reliance, and works actively with the non-profit WTI Inc., and other non-profits for the goals of urban sustainability. He can be reached at www.SchoolofSelf-Reliance.com, or Box 41834, Eagle Rock, CA 90041.

INDEX